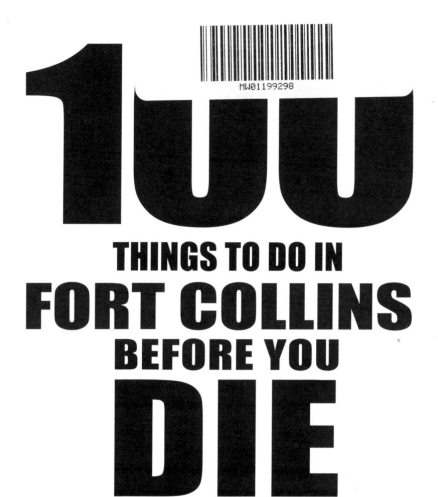

100
THINGS TO DO IN
FORT COLLINS
BEFORE YOU
DIE

100

THINGS TO DO IN
FORT COLLINS
BEFORE YOU
DIE

• •

DEBORAH BOUZIDEN

REEDY PRESS

Library of Congress Control Number: 2020937340

ISBN: 9781681062686

Design by Jill Halpin

Photos by author unless otherwise noted.

Printed in the United States of America
20 21 22 23 24   5 4 3 2 1

DEDICATION

This book is dedicated to all the people of Fort Collins for their commitment and willingness to make their city the best it can be, all the shop and restaurant owners, managers, and workers, and the known and unknown musicians who bring Fort Collins alive on the weekends and during festivals. And finally, this book is dedicated to my daughter, Yolanda, who is always encouraging me to "try" new things and is willing to go on new adventures with me every time I am ready.

CONTENTS

Music and Entertainment

• •

Sports and Recreation

Culture and History

• •

• •

ACKNOWLEDGMENTS

Books like these would not be possible without the help of the whole community. In the middle of the writing of this book, the COVID-19 Pandemic of 2020 struck and everyone in the country was placed in some level of quarantine. Businesses were shut down, and for those that remained in operation, takeout or mail order was the only option. Despite the difficulties the Pandemic presented, the people of Fort Collins came together to help make this book happen.

I would like to thank all the museum directors and shop and restaurant owners and managers who were kind enough to offer their time and voices to this project. I would like to offer a special thank you to Jeff Haber of Sage Hospitality, musician Stevey Ertl, and Tom McLellan, man-about-town and admirer of all things Fort Collins.

On the days I was out and about, I was reminded that Fort Collins is a truly hospitable, caring, and giving community. Residents are deeply warmhearted individuals who want to see their community safe, enduring, and thriving. When you come to visit, know you are entering not only a community, but a family. I hope when you leave, Fort Collins will remain on your heart and in your mind. Plan to return often, sit down in the restaurants, eat meals, shop in the stores, visit the museums, and enjoy all the outdoor activities this wonderful town has to offer. I will see you here.

• •

PREFACE

Fort Collins, also called "Fort" by many of the locals, sits 65 miles north of Denver, up I-25, and about 44 minutes south of Cheyenne, Wyoming. Home to Colorado State University, it is a college town, and during the school term Fort is alive with students and visiting parents. However, during the summer students leave and the city becomes a playground for visitors and locals. It is a happening place, and people from all around the area flock here to get good food, enjoy a brew or two, and shop in its unique and interesting stores.

Before Fort Collins was built in 1862, native tribes like the Arapaho and fur traders from every country crisscrossed the area. When travelers and early settlers along the Overland Trail asked for protection, the ninth Kansas Volunteer Calvary built Camp Collins here to serve that need. Even though the fort itself closed three years later, in 1877 the railroad came through the small remaining settlement that consisted of a hotel, general store, school, and post office. From there the town grew and expanded into what it is today, keeping the name of that first cavalry camp. In 1978, the town was placed on the National Register of Historic Places for its historical importance in the region.

Today Fort Collins continues to pulse with a kind of frontier excitement and an explosion of modern activities. In 2018, its population numbered over 171,000 residents with approximately

34,000 added when college classes started. Thus, the town maintains a teeming roster of daytime activities and a lively social night life.

With an average of 300 days of sunshine to work with, Fort Collins residents are always ready and willing to explore the outdoors. In the summer one can hike, bike, boat, fish, or swim. There is the Cache La Poudre River, Horsetooth Reservoir, and the entrance to the Rocky Mountain National Park only about an hour's drive west. In the winter, residents spend time snowshoeing close by, exploring the downtown area, and attending some of the many festivals the town has to offer.

Crammed into its 60 square miles, there are parks for throwing Frisbees, benches for sitting and people-watching, restaurants serving everything from chicken fried steak to sushi, and–if you enjoy music–many places to hear jazz or modern country wafting out the front door. Shopping opportunities are abundant and you can find everything from stores where you can blend your own tea or spices to places for picking out various flavored olive oils. I enjoy the cheese factories, wineries, and bookstores myself, but there are also breweries and bakeries that shouldn't be missed. With the Budweiser Center close by, visitors can catch shows and concerts at night after enjoying brew tours and trolley rides through town during the day.

Historic tours as well as ghost tours are available. Brew tours are plentiful and visits to local sourcing farms are just a short drive away. Fort Collins has something happening all year round and you will definitely be able to find *100 Things to Do in Fort Collins Before You Die* and much more.

● ●

Photo courtesy of the Waltzing Kangaroo

FOOD AND DRINK

TAKE A TRIP TO THAILAND
AT CAFÉ DE BANGKOK

For authentic Thai food, look no further than Café de Bangkok Fort Collins. Close to the university, this restaurant transports you to another world with its Thai-speaking chefs and open kitchen design. Customers can peek inside to watch native chefs prepare authentic Thai cuisine and listen to kitchen noises that resonate with Thai culture.

Don't worry: You don't have to speak Thai to eat here. You just have to love the food.

The restaurant doesn't sell alcohol, but they do sell the best Pad Thai, Pad Se-Ew, and Drunken Noodles in the state according to patrons. Kao Soi, a dish from Northern Thailand that includes flat noodles and chicken slow-cooked in red curry soup and garnished with pickles, shallots, and lime, is another local favorite. Ingredients are the freshest to be found, and some–like Holy Basil–come from Thailand itself.

So, if your mouth is watering just thinking about all the wonderful Asian flavors, head on in. Let co-owner Nattatida "Kae" Dumrongpalasit and her staff show you the taste of real Thai food.

1232 W Elizabeth St. C-7, 970-672-8127, cafedebangkokfoco.com

GO WEST YOUNG MAN, BUT STOP
AT THE FORKS MERCANTILE AND SALOON

If you're out for a day trip and want a little western spice in your life, head west out of Fort Collins to The Forks Mercantile and Saloon which provides an especially good reason to visit Livermore, Colorado.

The Forks used to be a stagecoach stop back in the day, but now it's a great place to meet up as a destination. Upstairs is the saloon where you can play pool, get a drink, or do a little dancin'. One of the heaping baskets of fries, onion rings, or fried pickle chips alone would fill you up, but don't pass on the burgers. The Forks Burger is my favorite, while my daughter likes either the 287 or the Bronco Burger with jalapeños.

Downstairs in the Saloon, you can order pizza, a sandwich from the deli, or one of The Forks ice cream treats like floats, malts, or cones. In the Mercantile section, you can also pick up a few essentials like bread, milk, and ice, or pay for the gas that you pumped out front.

Before you leave, sit and relax a spell in one of the classic rocking chairs or swings. Watch the sun go down or come up. The Forks is a one-stop, must-stop shop.

17685 US-287, 970-472-2690, forksmercantile.com

FINE DINING IN A RELAXED ATMOSPHERE
AT SONNY LUBICK STEAKHOUSE

For a special dining experience, go to Sonny Lubick Steakhouse. Named for Sonny Lubick, the highly regarded and beloved football coach of the Colorado State University Rams, this restaurant perpetuates his legacy by not only serving some of the finest food in town, but also by giving patrons a warm hometown feel.

You can order steaks made the way you like them. Add a few sides, an adult beverage, and you'll be set for the evening. If you enjoy a good wine with your meal, Sonny Lubick's has the most renowned wine cellar in Northern Colorado. Be sure to order a serving of the Crème Brûlée, Walrus Ice Cream, or Sonny's Butter Cake before you leave.

It's wise to make a reservation before you go. The easiest way is to visit the restaurant's website and book your table there. Live music is available on Friday and Saturday nights from 8 p.m. to 11 p.m. So, what are you waiting for? Go check it out!

115 S College Ave., 970-484-9200, sonnylubicksteakhouse.com

COME CELEBRATE FUN
AT GINGER AND BAKER

Not a special occasion? Not to worry. Anytime is a great time to visit Ginger and Baker. It's more than a restaurant; it's the happening place to be. You can eat, shop, or cook here. It's a trifecta of fun.

You can have amazing fruit or chicken pie, and you'll be eating it in an equally amazing historical setting. The building used to be a grain mill and feed barn providing services to local farmers. Now, it's on the National Register of Historic places as well as a place of business.

Ginger and Baker is a hub for the community located in the River District of Fort Collins. Besides the Café, there's the Market & Bakery, Teaching Kitchen, Rooftop Bar, Wine Cellar, Mill Top Event Space, and The Cache restaurant and bar which features Colorado-inspired dishes made with local beef, bison, fish, produce, and more.

So, come for the food. Stay for the fun.

359 Linden St., 970-223-7437, gingerandbaker.com

"SEA" SOME FIREWORKS
AT WHITE TREE

Opened in October 2016, White Tree restaurant is a local favorite. Serving sushi items like sashimis, nigiris, or its signature roll, White Tree always offers patrons something to love. After all, everything on the menu is served at its freshest.

This place has many repeat customers whether they're coming for the Las Vegas deep fried roll, Bulgoggi salad bowl, or the Fireworks Roll which is lit on fire with rum before being brought to your table.

Besides eating the good food, patrons can hear excellent jazz music here several nights a week, and the Asian-style murals on the walls were done by the owner herself.

1015 S Taft Hill Rd., 970-286-2417, whitetree-sushi.com

CHEESE LOVERS UNITE
AT THE FOX AND THE CROW

Nationally recognized as "one of the best cheese shops in the nation," The Fox and The Crow offers a unique restaurant experience for customers of all ages. This casual bistro has a loyal base ranging from college students to the retiree. Women especially love coming here for girls' night out, but men are encouraged to visit as well.

Cheese and meat boards are standard here, but if you like sandwiches, you will be pleased to know that the restaurant bakers make their own bread in-house. Soups are also made from scratch every day and the homemade mac and cheese is a favorite. While enjoying a charcuterie treat, cool off with a glass of wine, cider, or a local beer or Kombucha.

Classes where one can learn about all different kinds of cheese are offered once a month. They are limited to 20 participants and fill up quickly, so if you're interested, call in advance to reserve your space. If you can't make a class, don't worry. There are plenty of "cheesemongers" in the shop who can answer questions and help out with anything you need.

2601 S Lemay Ave., Unit 9, 970-999-2229, thefoxandthecrow.net

LET IT ROLL
AT THE SILVER GRILL CAFE

Looking for the biggest, baddest, and ooey-gooeyiest cinnamon roll in the West? Look no further than the Silver Grill Cafe. The café's history dates back to 1912, making it the oldest restaurant in Northern Colorado. Its homemade cinnamon rolls, which got their start in 1979, are legendary. A delectable sweet-craver's delight for young and old, the rolls measure one-and-a-quarter inch thick and five inches across the middle.

Known for the more than 10,000 cinnamon rolls it serves a month, the café is open for breakfast, brunch, lunch, and by special request in the evenings. The home-style cooking menu ranges from breakfast burritos and tacos for breakfast to cold meatloaf sandwiches and chicken fried chicken with mashed potatoes and gravy for lunch. Everybody will find a favorite here.

218 Walnut St., 970-484-4656, silvergrill.com

OTHER RESTAURANTS FOR YOU TO CHECK OUT

Avogadro's Number
605 S Mason St., 970-493-5555, avogadros.com

Butters AM Eatery
1103 W Elizabeth St., 970-797-2060
buttersbreakfast.com

Illegal Pete's Fort Collins
320 Walnut St., 970-999-3051, illegalpetes.com

JAWS Sushi
1205 W Elizabeth St., 970-682-2678, jawsfoco.com

La Creperie & French Baker
2722 S College Ave., 970-224-2640
fortcollinscreperiebakery.com

La Luz Mexican Grill
140 E Boardwalk Dr., 970-267-9444
laluzmexicangrill.com

Sherpa Grill 2
1501 W Elizabeth St. Unit 5, 970-893-2760
sherpagrill2togo.com

Simmer Fort Collins
2519 S Shields St. #1F, 970-893-2817, simmerfc.com

The Still Whiskey Steaks
151 N College Ave., 970-294-4360
thestillwhiskeysteaks.com

Tasty Harmony
160 W Oak St., 970-689-3234, tastyharmony.com

EXPERIENCE SMELLS, SOUNDS, AND TASTES
AT TASTE OF FORT COLLINS

When Summer arrives in Fort Collins, so do the festivals. That means food, fun, and frolicking, and there's no better place to find all three than the Taste of Fort Collins. Held on the first weekend in June in downtown Fort Collins's Civic Center and Washington Park, this three-day event is the place to be.

Food vendors with booths and trucks are on the premises along with breweries and other Colorado spirit vendors. Besides food and drink, there is live music for all three days and local artists have booths for you to wander through as well.

The event benefits the Eye Openers Kiwanis Club of Fort Collins, so while you may be visiting to have fun, you can also feel good about helping others while you are at it. Visit the website to learn more: tasteoffortcollins.com

Civic Center and Washington Park, tasteoffortcollins.com

ENJOY SWEET TREATS DELUXE
AT THE LITTLE BIRD BAKE SHOP

Celebrating their tenth year of business, this woman-owned establishment had made its mark on Fort Collins. The Little Bird Bake Shop is a bright little café with a homey, cozy vibe that has a very loyal group of regulars. Some come for the Crème Fraiche Quiche, while others enjoy the croissants, which come in different kinds like butter, almond, and chocolate. From bread to pies this bakery does it all for its customers.

Pastries may be the mainstay here, but they also serve specialty coffee drinks like Harbinger and Boxcar Coffee, as well as local Chai and unique tea blends. Summer visitors can try the Lavender Lemonade, which is superb.

All items on the menu are made from scratch, even the yogurt. They use pure, natural, and–when available–local ingredients. Bakers at the Little Bird Bake Shop start making dough in the wee hours of the morning so they can serve their customers the very finest and freshest products.

11 Old Town Square, Unit 121, 970-568-8906, thelittlebirdbakeshop.com

EXPERIENCE MORE THAN ONE EXPECTS
AT NICK'S ITALIAN

Guests, young and old, love going to Nick's Italian in Fort Collins. Besides a large wine list, the atmosphere is warm and friendly with an expansive patio for outside dining. Besides the usual Italian fare like lasagna and eggplant parmesan, Nick's also makes New York-style pizza and burgers. As a matter of fact, Nick's won "Best Burger" in Fort Collins out of 80 restaurants.

A lot of locals come here on Friday nights for clams and for the Saturday night prime rib. They have a full bar serving beverages from local beers to handcrafted cocktails.

Located across from the Colorado State University track and field complex, Nick's sponsors the annual Pizza Mile. It is a relay race where each member of a team of four eats a slice of pizza then runs 400 meters around the local high school track. Proceeds go to a local charity.

In true Italian style, Nick's keeps it interesting.

1100 S College Ave., 970-631-8301, nicksfc.com

GO BACK TO THE FUTURE AND BEYOND
AT TOTALLY 80'S PIZZA AND MUSEUM

The world's only 1980s pop culture museum, Totally 80's Pizza and Museum will blast you back to the past in a 1980s sort of way. The restaurant offers pizza, of course, with the usual toppings, but if guests want a little more adventure there are unique toppings to try like flaming hot Cheetos, cream cheese, Fritos, and tater tots.

Once visitors have had their fill of pizza, they wander back to the museum. Memorabilia from the *A-Team*, *Back to the Future, Teenage Mutant Ninja Turtles*, *Star Wars*, Pe-Wee Herman films, and too many 80's nostalgia items to mention can be found here. It doesn't matter if guests were around during that time and just want to take a walk down memory lane or if they're just curious, there will be something in the museum that will make them go "Hmmmm . . . ."

Special events like Colorado's largest Delorean Car Show, Ghostbusters Day, and Star Wars Day have guests coming not only from across the state, but from across the country as well. "We traveled from south Texas and made it a point to come here," a guest commented. "This place is amazing!"

1717 S College Ave., 970-867-5309, totally80spizza.com

GET MORE CHEESE PLEASE
AT CHEESE IMPORTERS

Located about 40 minutes south of Fort Collins on Highway 287 and just across the railroad tracks in Longmont, Colorado, visitors will find the Cheese Importers. This unique French-style bistro offers both restaurant and retail shopping experiences. The old two-story brick building is perfect for what is tucked inside. Visitors can enjoy eating freshly baked French baguettes, straight from France, but baked on-site, or feast on a slice of Quiche Lorraine. The bistro also serves salads, sandwiches, soups, almond croissants, and a bevy of other sweet treats. The Rose Lemonade is a special treat and perfect for sipping out on the patio on a hot summer's day.

Whether or not you came for a meal, visitors need to check out the store merchandise brought in from France, England, and Italy. From there, grab a coat and step into the cheese cooler. One can sample cheeses from around the world and then purchase any favorites. There are enough olives, meats, and cheeses here to satisfy any palate. It is truly a one-of-a-kind experience.

103 Main St., Longmont, Colorado, 303-772-9599, cheeseimporters.com

STOP FOR FUNKY FOOD
AT B & B PICKLE BARREL

Just across the street from the college sits the B & B Pickle Barrel. Brenda and Bob started it 33 years ago after both attending Colorado State University. Brenda had worked for a popular restaurant and Bob worked in a butcher shop in New York and neither were impressed by the skimpy amounts of meat found in the sandwiches around town. With a loan from Bob's dad the sandwich shop was opened. It's a quirky little place with a mural on the wall, loud music, an open concept, and a small bar.

College kids help run the place and Brenda wouldn't have it any other way. She says they keep the place young and it needs to be that way with the sandwiches served here which have names like the Toonces, Funky Punky, Lucy's Delight, and Tobin's Tummy Pleaser. The breads for the sandwiches are made locally and delivered daily. Soups and stews, quiche, and the ever-popular mac and cheese are made daily. It can get busy during football season, but you should go ahead and stop in–if for nothing else, to try the Pickle Martini. It's something you won't soon forget.

122 W Laurel St., 970-484-0235, picklebarrelfc.com

YOU'LL FIND
THE RIGHT STUFF
AT THE EMPORIUM:
AN AMERICAN BRASSERIE

Despite a rebranding in 2020, this French-style bistro still offers attention to detail and a warm, easy feeling in a relaxed authentic atmosphere. At the Emporium: An American Brasserie you can eat breakfast, brunch, lunch, and dinner, seven days a week. The food is fresh here and diners can find everything from salads to the Emporium's signature items like Bison Bourguignon, Bouillabaisse, and Steak and Frites.

Located in the historic Elizabeth Hotel, the bistro delights visitors with its unique architectural touches, like the ceiling which looks like old tiles. All this adds to the European atmosphere. When dinner is over, the Kitchen and Wine Market is a must-visit. Here you will find the perfect wine to take home, perhaps the right cheese and meat for your own charcuterie platter and a board to go with it. The Emporium truly is a destination that people go to not just go through.

378 Walnut St., 970-493-0024, emporiumfc.com

FOR FOOD AND FUN

Every third Friday of the month, Fort Collins offers the Fort Collins Foodie Walk, a very popular Fort Collins event, highlighting a select group of Old Town's finest eateries. Twelve specialty food shops like The Cupboard, Kilwins Chocolates and Ice Cream, Mountain Avenue Market, and Nuance Chocolate, to name a few, stay open late to let "foodies" come and experience their culinary delights, get questions answered, and discover a little more about food and drink.

TIP

For information of happenings in Downtown Fort Collins (a.k.a. Old Town), you can sign up for News from Downtown from the Downtown Fort Collins Business Association. Visit their website at downtownfortcollins.com.

FIND A GOOD DAY, MATE
AT WALTZING KANGAROO

Hungry for something a little different or craving some cuisine from down under? Hop into Waltzing Kangaroo, where Australian chefs will cook up iconic Aussie dishes for patrons to enjoy. Everything here is made from scratch and diners will tell you the mashed potatoes will rival your grandma's. While they do make quiches, rolls, and sweets, the stars of the show here are the meat, vegetable, and dessert pies. You will want to try them all eventually, but start with the Steak and Gravy pie, then move on to the Guinness, Steak, and Mushroom combination. There are 14 fillings altogether including the Chicken and White Cheese Sauce pie or the Madras Curry Chicken. Breakfast and dessert are served here as well; the Chocolate Pecan Tart is to die for. Come on down. What are you waiting for, mate?

1109 W Elizabeth St., 970-568-8817, waltzingkangaroo.com

DISCOVER WHERE EVERYBODY KNOWS YOUR NAME
AT MOOT HOUSE

For an intimate, relaxing, jolly-good time, look no further than the Moot House. This English-style pub is all about local flavors, literally. Twenty-five years ago, the owners wanted to create a community atmosphere where patrons could come, sit by the fire, enjoy a beer, or two, and visit with friends and family. They accomplished that and more. The owners purchase from vendors in the community and serve up to 30 craft beers on tap. Come here for brunch, which features Bread Pudding French Toast and several different types of Eggs Benedict. Pretzel rolls are a favorite, so be sure to order yours before they're sold out, which happens on a daily basis. Lunch and dinner times are always busy, so you might want to make a reservation.

2626 S College Ave., 970-226-2121, themoothouse.com

EXPERIENCE A LITTLE CUP OF HEAVEN
AT BUTTER CREAM CUPCAKERY

Hungry for dessert but don't want an entire cake? Check out Butter Cream Cupcakery. While they do serve coffee, tea, milk, and a few other drinks, cupcakes are the specialty here. There are seven different flavors per day: five everyday flavors including chocolate, vanilla, and red velvet, with a flavor of the day like lemon or almond, and then a surprise flavor. All of the cupcakes are made fresh every morning and contain no trans fats. Typically, on Thursday there is even a gluten-free option. You can buy one, half a dozen, a dozen, or even more. They do not ship their cupcakes, but GrubHub will deliver if you can't get in to pick up your own. Cupcakes are an excellent any-time-of-day treat so feel free to have one…or two.

172 N College Ave., 970-482-2505, buttercreamcupcakery.com

IT'S A GREAT DAY FOR ¡OLÉ!
AT RIO GRANDE MEXICAN RESTAURANT

The name Rio Grande Mexican Restaurant is all you need to know to find great Mexican food in downtown Fort Collins. First, you will want to try a margarita. There are several different kinds here, but go slow. The tequila, which is added generously, can sneak up on you. Second, they make their own tortillas so getting them fresh is a bonus. Chips and salsa flow freely while waiting for your meal. Besides the guacamole, the crab and shrimp enchiladas are a must-try. There are a few gluten-free offerings here, but if you don't find something you like on the menu, the staff will try to accommodate you as best they can. Service is friendly, but sometimes there is a wait as this restaurant is very popular. If possible, sit on the patio out back. There is a nice little fountain to enjoy while sipping on your adult beverage. Finally, try the churros for dessert to top off your dining experience.

143 W Mountain Ave., 970-224-5428, riograndemexican.com

COME IN AND EXPERIENCE NEW ORLEANS
AT LUCILE'S CREOLE CAFE

You don't have to go all the way to New Orleans to get authentic Cajun or Creole cuisine. In Fort, all you have to do is visit Lucile's Creole Cafe. Open for breakfast and lunch, you will find Eggs Pontchartrain, Gumbo, and Shrimp Creole to name but a few of the dishes on the menu. If you like it hot, check out the Hot Louisiana Andouille or Country Sausage. The buttermilk biscuits and grits are a staple here and if you come to Lucile's, you shouldn't leave without trying the beignets. They are New Orleans–style donuts, deep fried, sprinkled with powdered sugar, and served hot. Southern-style service is the norm here; for example, when you request orange or grapefruit juice, it will be squeezed fresh at your table by your waiter.

400 Meldrum St., 970-224-5464, luciles.com

GO OUT OF THIS WORLD
AT COMET CHICKEN

Located in one of the older brick buildings right off College Avenue, across from Walrus Ice Cream, is Comet Chicken. This restaurant is always busy because they have the best chicken in town based on the number of people who eat here or get their orders to go. Comet cooks always start with fresh, antibiotic-free chicken and hand-dip it into the batter after it is ordered. The result is a moist and tender delicacy. You can get chicken strips here or you can order one of their chicken sandwiches. Bring your appetite, though–the chicken portion is so big it hangs off the bun. The restaurant offers eight different types of dipping sauces including their House Sauce which is a mixture of ranch, honey mustard, and chipotle flavors. If you want your fries spicy, order the Space Fries. Otherwise, stick to the regular ones. They also have salads here, but no beef or pork–just chicken.

126 W Mountain Ave., 970-689-3464, cometchicken.com

SIZE DOES MATTER
AT BIG AL'S BURGERS AND DOGS

Whether you're hungry for a burger or a hot dog, you'll find both here at Big Al's Burgers and Dogs. This small hole-in-the-wall food establishment is big on taste and generous portions. The burgers are all homemade and served with the house sauce, tomato, lettuce, onions, and pickles, or you can order just meat and a bun. Hot dogs come oversized for the bun and one order of their hand-cut fries is enough to feed two people.

Besides the food, you'll love the atmosphere at Big AL's. Local artists' work decorates the walls with bright colors and a style unique to Fort Collins. College students hang out here a lot and on Friday and Saturday afternoons while school is in session the little restaurant fills up fast. Bring your patience and expect a good time.

140 W Mountain Ave., 970-232-9815, bigalsburgersanddogs.com

LAND HERE FOR SOME GOOD EATS
AT BUTTERFLY CAFE

Although this little building may not look like much, inside is a place where great coffee and unique signature food is served. In only 400 square feet, the Butterfly Cafe offers up a unique and satisfying dining experience. It serves one-of-a-kind mochas, lattes, sandwiches, breakfast foods like breakfast tacos and burritos, and some of the best pastries in town according to loyal customers. There are many vegetarian options here as their motto is that healthy food is good food. There are a few seats inside, but there is also patio seating outside. If the seating is a little cramped for you, you can always get your order to go. This little spot is located in the historic Butterfly House and is only open for breakfast and lunch. Along with the food mentioned above, this craft kitchen makes soups, homemade bread for their sandwiches, and cookies and other pastries from scratch on the premises. The Butterfly Cafe is also known for their smoothies made from real fruit and their own almond milk.

212 Laporte Ave., 970-999-5793, butterflycafefortcollins.com

"BEER IS MADE BY MEN, WINE BY GOD"
... AND TEN BEARS WINERY
(MARTIN LUTHER)

And some of the wine at Ten Bears Winery is made by the grapes grown in Colorado in the winery's own vineyard. When the winery first opened back in 2007, the grapes were purchased from growers on Colorado's Western Slope. Gradually, winery owners decided to start growing grapes of their own, so in 2009, 480 vines were planted. Today, the winery makes over 20 different varieties of wine including: their whites–Altitude Sparkling, Helluva White, Roaming Bear Passion Fruit; their reds–Grand Valley Merlot, Larimer County Estate Marquette, Poudre Valley Red; and their dessert wines—Grand Valley Primitivo, Nutty Laporte, and Roaming Bear Pomegranate. If you like wine, you should visit the tasting room to find your favorite. Even though the tasting room is located about eight miles from downtown Fort Collins, you'll be glad you made the drive.

5114 County Rd. 23E, 970-566-4043, tenbearswinery.com

WINERIES AND DISTILLERIES
FOR YOU TO EXPLORE

Blue Skies Winery
251 Jefferson St., 970-407-9463, blueskyvineyard.com

Blendings at the Preserve
3924 Bingham Hill Rd., 970-889-3162, blendings.wine

The Infinite Monkey Theorem
234 N College Ave. A3, 512-271-6807
theinfinitemonkeytheorem.com

Sweetheart Winery
5500 W US-34, 970-646-4314, sweetheartwinery.com

Elevation 5003 Distillery
2601 S Lemay Ave., Unit 1, 970-568-8356
elevation5003.com

Feisty Spirits Distillery
1708 E Lincoln Ave. #1, 970-444-2386, feistyspirits.com

Mobb Mountain Distillers
400 Linden St., 970-689-3887, mobbmountain.com

Old Town Distilling Company
513 N Link Lane Unit E, 970-443-5668
oldtowndistilling.com

Old Elk Distillery
253 Linden St., 970-287-0640, oldelkdistillery.com

NOCO Distillery
328 Link Lane Court #11, 970-414-7188
nocodistillery.com

IT'S ALL IN THE POT
AT MELTING POT FORT COLLINS

If you want to have a unique dining experience, be sure to visit the Melting Pot in Fort Collins. Bring a friend or bring a lot of friends to sit around and enjoy laughs and good conversation, while reconnecting over artisan cheese fondues, salads, and luxurious desserts. Besides cheese fondues, there are entrée fondues that allow you to dip your favorite proteins or vegetarian choices in seasoned broth, a wine-based fondue, citrus dips, and then the ever-popular chocolate fondues which come in milk, dark, or white chocolate. There are a lot of drink choices from local beers and wines to specialty cocktails and spirit-free drinks like Blackberry Sage Lemonade and the Toothless Shark Bite. For those who need gluten-free options, not to worry. Your waiter will help you make some great choices. Stopping by here after a busy time of shopping, sightseeing, or hiking will make the end of a perfect day.

334 E Mountain Ave., 970-207-0100, meltingpot.com

ENJOY AN EDUCATIONAL EXPERIENCE
AT COPPERMUSE DISTILLERY

After touring the wineries and breweries, you might want to check out CopperMuse Distillery and take one of their free tours to learn about the hard liquor distilling process. There are no "free" samples, but you will learn a lot about making artisan spirits from beginning to end. You can purchase a cocktail to sip while you go on the tour to get a taste of the quality libations found here. After the tour, be sure to check out the vodkas, rums, whiskeys, and liqueurs in the on-site store. Customers claim that the CopperMuse rum and amaretto are the best around. They also sell kits, baskets, and other merchandise like T-shirts and copper mule cups. Located downtown in Old Town, this is another "must-stop."

244 N College Ave. #105, 970-999-6016, coppermuse.com

EVERYBODY LOVES ICE CREAM
AT WALRUS ICE CREAM

After eating some Comet Chicken, stop in at Walrus Ice Cream for more local fare. Unique to Fort Collins, this ice cream parlor uses only the freshest ingredients and makes all their ice cream on the premises. Current owners, John and Lisa Pugh purchased the existing store in 1999 and moved to their current location. They are proud to be part of the happiest times in people's lives, celebrating birthdays, graduations, first dates, or just enjoying family time together.

Since they do make their own ice cream, they are always introducing new flavors. Their ice cream base comes from a local dairy and they use real fruit from local vendors like the popular ice cream made with Palisade peaches. They use Coopersmith's Root Beer for their floats, and they collaborate with other businesses to offer unique flavors. They make their own cookie dough, whipped cream, hand-dipped ice cream sandwiches, and chocolate-covered bananas. Given that they also make their own ice cream cake, they can fulfill almost any request within 48 hours.

As Lisa says, "Any time is a good time for ice cream," so be sure to stop in frequently to sample all their flavors.

125 W Mountain Ave., 970-482-5919, walrusicecream.com

DO A BREW TOUR,
BUT START AT NEW BELGIUM BREWING COMPANY

Visitors to Fort Collins won't want to miss this employee-owned brewery located on Brewery Row. New Belgium Brewery Company started in the Fort Collins basement of co-founders Kim Jordan and Jeff Lebesch in 1991 after a biking trip through Belgium, and today it is the fourth-largest craft brewer in the United States. Now, the focus is not only on their beers, but on their employees. Locals contend that "Getting a job here is in as much demand as getting a tour."

Known as one of the best breweries in Fort Collins, spaces in New Belgium's 90-minute brew tours fill up fast. Tours here are free, so you will need to reserve a spot online days before you visit. You will not only get to sample their sour beers but will also see how their Fat Tire and award-winning Abbey ales are made. Another must-see on the tour are the large French oak wooden barrels used for fermenting and aging the beers. Visitors are so impressed by the craftsmanship and friendliness at this brewery that they often order a brew and grab a bite to eat from one of the food trucks that come daily in order to stay longer relaxing on the spacious outdoor patio.

500 Linden St., 970-221-0524, newbelgium.com

GET YOUR TWO WHEELIN' FUN ON
AT NEW BELGIUM'S TOUR DE FAT

Every September, New Belgium Brewery holds its combined parade and bike ride. Many participants are repeaters and they range from locals, out-of-town guests, and of course, New Belgium coworkers. Besides participating in the event, many employees also volunteer. The parade and bike ride are opportunities for participants to dress up and ride in the parade while showing off their favorite persona. In 2019, the event hosted a contest for best parade float. The winners received a gift card to the brewery and bragging rights. The parade consists of comedians, cirque performers, musicians, and employees of New Belgium Brewing Company.

Launched in 2000, New Belgium's Tour de Fat is a "celebration of great beer, good people, and humankind's most wonderful invention–the bicycle." This philanthropic festival has raised over $6 million for local bike nonprofit organizations. There is never a fee to participate. All proceeds are donated.

This is truly a celebration for the entire city and people love attending. Guests come from across the country and you should too. Check out their website under "Events" for the exact weekend.

Downtown Fort Collins, 970-221-0524, newbelgium.com

HOP ON IN
FOR THE BREW TOURS
AT MAGIC BUS TOURS AND BEER
AND BIKE TOURS

Fort Collins is known as the Craft Beer Capital of Colorado because of the 20-plus craft breweries located here. While you can most certainly create your own itinerary by visiting the breweries on your own, why risk missing a gem when you can get a tour, learn about different beer styles and the history of brewing in Fort Collins, and get delivered right to the doors of these breweries all at the same time?

Magic Bus Tours, located in downtown Fort Collins, offers walkabout tours, Magic Bus Cruise tours, or a four-hour private excursion to four breweries including New Belgium, Odell, Horse and Dragon, Coopersmith's, and more. Just call them up to make the arrangements.

Another avenue you might want to investigate is the Beer and Bike Tours. Here you hop on a bike and go from brewery to brewery. You can go on a day tour around Fort Collins or plan a longer trip around Colorado from the tour's base in Fort Collins.

Magic Bus Tours, 970-420-0662, themagicbustours.com

Beer and Bike Tours, 2414 Stanley Court, 970-201-1085
beerandbiketours.com

BREWERIES AROUND TOWN

Black Bottle Brewery
1611 S College Ave., 970-493-2337
blackbottlebrewery.com

Horse & Dragon Brewing Company
124 Racquette Dr., 970-631-8038
horseanddragonbrewing.com

Funkwerks
1900 E Lincoln Ave. Unit B, 970-482-3865
funkwerks.com

Odell Brewing Company
800 E Lincoln Ave., 970-498-9070, odellbrewing.com

Crooked Stave Fort Collins
225 Pine St., 970-999-5856, crookedstave.com

Jessup Farm Barrel House
1921 Jessup Dr., 970-568-8345
jessupfarmbarrelhouse.com

Coopersmith's Pub and Brewing
5 Old Town Square, 970-498-0483
coopersmithpub.com

Photo courtesy of Stevey Ertl

MUSIC AND ENTERTAINMENT

CHECK TO SEE IF YOU AIN'T AFRAID OF NO GHOSTS
DURING FORT COLLINS GHOST TOURS

Every town has its hauntings; you just need to know where to look. So, if you like to shake things up and get a little spooky, check out the Fort Collins Ghost Tours. These tours take you into the tunnels under Old Town Fort Collins while regaling you with stories about ghosts, local legends, and other bizarre happenings.

Tours are given year-round, but there is an age restriction because of the tours' subject matter. Of course, October is their busiest time so be prepared to book well in advance if that is your tour time of choice. Tours last approximately an hour and a half and you can book online. Just remember: these are walking tours in city tunnels so wear comfortable, closed-toe footwear.

19 Old Town Square, 970-372-1445, fortcollinstours.com

TIP

Be sure to check out the other tour topics offered by the Fort Collins Tours company: Speakeasies and Spirits, Ghosts and Goodies, Haunted Pub, and Late-Night Ghost.

HAPPY DAYS ARE HERE AGAIN
AT THE HOLIDAY TWIN DRIVE-IN

Remember the good old days of Friday and Saturday night drive-ins where you could sit in your car and enjoy a movie or two without bumping into anyone? From March to October, the Holiday Twin Drive-In still provides that nostalgic feeling, complete with the latest blockbuster movies. Located northwest of Fort Collins near Horsetooth Reservoir, the Holiday Twin offers two movies a night to watch in the privacy of your own car for half the price of a regular theater ticket. No getting elbowed, no people crawling over you, or spilling your drink or popcorn. You drive in, park your car, tune your radio to the Drive-In frequency, go get something to eat and drink from the concession stand, and enjoy this comfortable and nostalgic experience.

The Holiday Twin Drive-In has two screens, so you've got a choice of movies. The snack bar sells burgers, nachos, and the usual popcorn, along with other movie snacks and drinks for drive-in patrons.

It is possible to buy tickets online with a credit card, but if you want to get them at the box office there, bring cash.

2206 S Overland Trail, 970-221-1244, holidaytwin.com

CATCH SOME RAYS
IN THE SUNSET LOUNGE

In the mood for a drink, some good music, and a good time with friends? Look no further than the Sunset Lounge. Sitting on top of the Elizabeth Hotel, this rooftop lounge is a nice place to gather, have a cocktail, and listen to some jazz music. The lounge will only accommodate about 50 people, so the experience is an intimate one. While visitors go there for the music and adult beverages, an added attraction is the view. It's a great place to watch the sun set or activities in downtown Old Fort Collins. In the winter, guests can see Fort Collins lit up for the Christmas season. The whole town becomes covered in silent snow like a storybook setting and you can enjoy it all from the warmth and comfort of the lounge.

111 Chestnut St., 970-999-3494, sunsetloungerooftop.com

DIVE INTO A GOOD TIME
AT THE MAGIC RAT

If you're in town and are just looking to relax with an adult beverage and some music, visit the Magic Rat. Some have described this place as a dive, but it is more of an intimate lounge. There is live music here and artists range from well-known musicians to talented, up-and-coming artists. Music starts around 8 p.m. and there is a dance floor if you feel like getting your jiggy on. Eating a meal before you come is a good idea: while they do serve some food items like pizza and hot dogs, mostly it's wine, beer, and cocktails. No need to dress up, but if you are in a tux or silk, that's okay too. The Magic Rat is a come-as-you-are place.

111 Chestnut St. Firehouse Alley, 970-493-4120, magicratlivemusic.com

STAY AT THE ELIZABETH HOTEL, A HOTEL WITH SOUL...
AND A LOT OF ROCK 'N ROLL

While in Fort Collins, visitors who love music will want to stay at the Elizabeth Hotel. With 164 rooms–three of them suites–guests will certainly find accommodations that suit them. From terraces to patios, this hotel satisfies the pickiest traveler. Inside each gorgeously decorated room, guests will find a record player. Visitors are encouraged to check out vinyl records from the Hotel's record library and play them on the turntable in the comfort of their rooms. If that isn't enough to entice guests to check in, the Instrument Lending Library will certainly stir some interest. Guests have a choice of stringed instruments like guitars, mandolins, banjos, bass, and ukuleles to check out and take to their rooms to play. A stay at the Elizabeth is a unique experience for any music lover. Located in Old Town Fort Collins, the Elizabeth Hotel puts you near all the action while still encouraging you to be a part of it.

111 Chestnut St., 970-490-2600, theelizabethcolorado.com

ENJOY
THE SOUND OF MUSIC
AT BOHEMIAN NIGHTS

If you love music (and who doesn't?), you might want to check out Bohemian Nights in downtown Fort Collins. Every summer–usually in August–for three days across six stages, 80 or more bands play continuously entertaining hundreds of fans young and old. Four stages are standing room only, while the Oak Street and Kids' Music Adventure Stages have seating. The music lineup is very diverse offering not only nationally known headliners, but new and local groups. While the concerts are free, there are a lot of specialty booths selling band merchandise, art, and food. This is also a great opportunity to find a new favorite band and learn about them and their music. If you want to bring the kids, don't worry. Their area is not only educational, but fun. The whole family is sure to have a good time here.

Downtown Fort Collins, 970-692-3788, bohemiannights.org

TIP

If you can't make it to the August event, you might catch one of the free Thursday night summer concerts this organization puts on. These concerts showcase some of Colorado's finest–not only the established musical artists, but up-and-coming bands as well.

Downtown Fort Collins
bohemiannights.org/thursday-night-live.html

EXPERIENCE SOMETHING OLD AND SOMETHING NEW
AT THE EDWARDS HOUSE

If you're looking for somewhere a little different, unique, and intimate, book your stay at The Edwards House. Built in 1904 for Alfred Augustus Edwards, this foursquare home was typical of the structures designed during that time period. It was built in the Neoclassical style with a large front porch and a hexagonal pergola on the east side. The Edwards family lived in this home until 1981. In 1993, it became a bed and breakfast.

Today, there are eight rooms for guests to choose from, all bright and cheery and ready for you to relax in and be pampered. Some of the amenities you will enjoy include a complimentary breakfast and refreshment station, soft and inviting bath robes, radiant heat bathroom floors, free parking, and–in select rooms–gas fireplaces.

402 W Mountain Ave., 970-493-9191, edwardshouse.com

TIP

Don't worry if you forget some of your personal items. Cedar & Sage Mercantile, The Edwards House sister store has everything you will need. From shampoo to toothbrushes, they are just a call or short walk away. You can also have these or any other items you may need delivered to your room.

WHERE COLOR AND MUSIC COLLIDE
DURING PIANOS ABOUT TOWN

What's more fun than a brightly painted piano? Someone playing that piano. Every summer, Fort Collins comes alive with music. In 2010, the City of Fort Collins Art in Public Places Program collaborated with the Bohemian Foundation and the Downtown Development Authority to put donated pianos into the hands of artists, both visual and musical. Artists gave their time to paint these pianos and then they were strategically placed around Fort Collins, not only for art lovers to enjoy, but for music lovers as well. Ten years later, the project is still going strong. The pianos are scattered around 20 locations throughout the summer and six locations in the winter so passersby can watch artists decorate the musical instruments and play a tune if they are so inspired. According to the Pianos About Town organization, these pianos are "interactive public art"–just another unique thing about Fort Collins. Even if all you know is "Twinkle, Twinkle, Little Star" or "Heart and Soul," you'll get a kick out of tickling these ivories on the streets of Fort Collins.

Downtown Fort Collins, 970-221-2636, fcgov.com/artspublic/pianos.php

HAVE AN EXPERIENCE IN THE ROUND
AT THE OTTERBOX DIGITAL DOME THEATER

Want to kick back, relax, and catch a show? Visit the Otterbox Digital Dome Theater. This theater is the only full-dome theater in northern Colorado. It features a 39-foot-diameter domed screen with 80 seats to give visitors an optimum 360-degree viewing experience. Topics are wide-ranging, and cover everything from space exploration to music concerts. The theater is a part of the Fort Collins Museum of Discovery and therefore is open when the museum is. Different programs are held throughout the year, but on Tune-Out Tuesday, you can bring your lunch and relax to soothing tunes and views of the cosmos. If you have small children, they will enjoy Storytime in the Dome. Designed for children seven and under, this storytime is followed by crafts in the Learning Lab.

408 Mason Court, 970-221-6738, fcmod.org/dometheater/

EXPLORE, LEARN, AND HAVE FUN
AT THE FORT COLLINS MUSEUM OF DISCOVERY

Two entities, the City of Fort Collins Museum and the non-profit Discovery Center, joined in 2008 to create the Fort Collins Museum of Discovery that visitors enjoy today. This museum mixes culture and science to create an educational experience unique to the Front Range.

Each year, they offer over 400 programs for all age groups. There is a 16,000-square-foot main exhibit that includes agriculture, astronomy, first peoples, music, and science, not to mention the Heritage Courtyard which focuses on local history and settlement. You can grab a bite to eat at the Museum Café or take a piece of your experience home with you from the gift shop.

If that isn't enough, Fort Collins Museum of Discovery has two live black-footed ferrets, one of the most endangered mammals in America, who make their home here. This is the only museum in the world to have living examples of these endangered North American mammals on display.

408 Mason Court, 970-221-6738, fcmod.org

HAVE A BACK-TO-NATURE CONCERT EXPERIENCE
AT MISHAWAKA AMPHITHEATRE

If you like outdoor music concerts, you need to check out Mishawaka Amphitheatre and the bands they host. Located along the Poudre River in the Canyon, this is a perfect place to hold a concert because of the way the sound travels. You will also find a full service restaurant here. Enjoy a beer and a burger out on the deck and watch for wildlife before the music starts. Be prepared: the concerts are standing room only and lawn chairs are only allowed if the venue is not sold out. Blankets are prohibited. Although there are camping areas close by, the parking lot charges a fee if you decide to drive there. The best option is to catch a shuttle bus from Colorado State University. It's a perfect venue for outdoor concert lovers.

13714 Poudre Canyon Hwy., 888-843-6474, themishawaka.com

SPORTS AND RECREATION

A WALK AROUND
AT COLORADO STATE UNIVERSITY

As with any college town, the educational institution plays a pivotal role in its makeup and livelihood. Fort Collins is no exception. Colorado State University is situated west of Old Town but is as much a centerpiece of Fort Collins as Old Downtown. The Colorado Agricultural School welcomed its first students on September 1, 1879. While the school started with one building known as "Old Main," between 1879 and 1954 more buildings were added around an oval green space where students and visitors still walk today. The 10 buildings comprising the Guggenheim Hall of Household Arts, Ammons Hall, Morgan Library Building, and Danforth Chapel have all been renovated. However, many have restored woodwork which represents the time period of their construction. The buildings are in daily use by the university but are still open to the public so visitors can enjoy their historical aspects. One walk around the oval allows visitors to not only appreciate its beautiful landscaping, but the human innovation as well.

Fort Collins, Colorado, 970-491-6444, colostate.edu

TIP

Colorado State University is home to the CSU Rams. While the football games are held in Canvas Stadium, there are also basketball, golf, track and field, tennis, volleyball, cross country, softball, swimming, and a host of other teams that call CSU home. The Rams are a lively bunch and their games are always a joy to watch. If you feel like cheering a team on, look no further than one of their Rams' games or activities.

FISH THE LITTLE FISHING HOLE
THAT IS HORSETOOTH RESERVOIR

Fifteen minutes west of Fort Collins is Horsetooth Reservoir. It is six-and-a-half miles long and for water pursuits, you couldn't ask for more. Named for the rock formation that sits above it, the reservoir offers boating, fishing, swimming, water skiing, and any number of other water activities. Because it is so close to Fort Collins, you can spend the day swimming and picnicking along the water and be back in time to catch a show in the evening in town. If you want to camp in a tent or trailer instead of staying in a hotel in town, these options are available to you as well. This recreation area is open all year round and is a good choice for any outdoor activity.

Larimer County, 970-679-4570

TIP
There are many trails and recreation areas around the Reservoir. One trail that is immensely popular is Arthur's Rock Trail. This trail leads up to Arthur's Rock, a great place to spend a morning or afternoon enjoying great vistas of the land all around.

MORE TO DO
AT HORSETOOTH MOUNTAIN
OPEN SPACE

A little farther west of the Reservoir is Horsetooth Mountain Open Space. This 2,711-acre area has 29 miles of hiking, biking, and horseback-riding trails. Most of them are rated easy to moderate for their respective sports and the running trails are well-known for being excellent places for runners to train.

Nature trips are popular in this area for all the wildflower, wildlife, and bird-watching opportunities. The views from the top of Horsetooth Mountain are spectacular and during the summer crowds of people may be gathered to watch the rising or setting sun.

Along one of the trails, you will want to stop and enjoy Horsetooth Falls. It is a short hike of 2.2 miles from the trailhead with a slight 393-foot elevation gain. The view is definitely worth the walk.

Whether you have all or only part of a day to hike, Horsetooth Mountain Open Space is a spectacular place to visit and enjoy. This area is open all year round but be aware that in the winter months, the trails may be icy and/or muddy. Dogs are allowed on most trails here, but they must be kept on leash.

6550 W County Rd. 38 E, 970-498-7000
larimer.org/naturalresources/parks/horsetooth-mountain

HIT THE TRAIL ... IN TOWN
ON POUDRE RIVER AND
SPRING CREEK TRAILS

Granted, when most people think of trails, they think rugged, off-road, and mountainous. There are two trails in Fort Collins that don't fit those descriptions, but will satisfy everyone.

The Poudre River Trail is 10 miles long and follows the Cache La Poudre River as it runs through Fort Collins. It starts at Lyons Park, west of Fort Collins, and ends on East Drake Avenue at the Environmental Learning Center. The trail has easy on/off access to Old Fort Collins, so hikers taking a leisurely stroll might want to stop for a brew along the way. Hearty souls who want to continue for another 11 miles can follow the trail all the way to Windsor and Greeley.

Spring Creek Trail runs from West Drake Road at Rolland Moore Park to the junction of Spring Creek and the Poudre River where it joins the Poudre River Trail. This trail is popular because it provides a link between the west and east sides of Fort Collins. Seven miles long, it cuts through several parks and then passes by the Gardens at Spring Creek where the Butterfly House and Botanical Garden are located.

Both trails are paved and provide a great way to spend a morning or afternoon no matter what the season.

For trail maps visit: Poudre River Trail Corridor, Inc., 1100 10th St., #210, 970-336-4044, poudretrail.org

Spring Creek Trail traillink.com, trail/spring-creek-trail-(co)

COOL OFF
IN THE SUMMER HEAT
AT POUDRE RIVER WHITEWATER PARK

If you'd rather cool off in a river than a lake, get on down to the Poudre River Whitewater Park. After 20 years and $11.5 million, the park opened in 2019. It has facilities for swimming, kayaking, and tubing. The water features may be man-made, but they are perfect for either those adventurers wanting to test their kayak skills or weekenders who just like to float in a tube. Along the banks are places for people to swim or have a picnic when hunger calls. The Poudre River flows through the park and the man-made features are designed to make the rapids safer and more accessible. There is a pedestrian bridge over the river, so visitors who don't want to sit on the banks of the river can watch all the activity from overhead. Even though this is a park, there are no lifeguards on duty and guests still need to use caution and follow safety rules when visiting the park. There are no kayak or tubing rentals on-site, but you can rent them from a local business or bring your own.

201 E Vine Dr., 970-221-6660, fcgov.com/parkplanning/poudre-river-park

BEAUTY IS IN THE EYE OF THE BEHOLDER
AT COYOTE RIDGE NATURAL AREA

At first glance, this trail may not look impressive, but looks can be deceiving. This short 2.3-mile natural trail in the Coyote Ridge Natural Area with its 600-foot elevation gain still offers an excellent workout for mountain bikers, hikers, horseback riders, and even walkers. The trail begins right off the parking lot which is located about three miles south of Harmony on the west side of Taft Hill Road. About a mile into the trail, there is a cabin where you can pick up information about the trail and that is where the quarter-mile interpretive loop starts and ends. Along the way, you can expect to see rabbits, deer mice, prairie dogs, mule deer, lizards, coyotes, songbirds, and even the occasional rattlesnake or mountain lion. If you choose to hike this trail, watch your step. Dogs are not allowed here.

This is a popular trail and parking spots fill up fast. There are only five horse-trailer spots, so please don't park in those areas. The best time to visit Coyote Ridge is in the morning as storms come over the ridge during the early to late afternoons.

Three miles south of Harmony on Taft Hill Rd., 970-416-2815

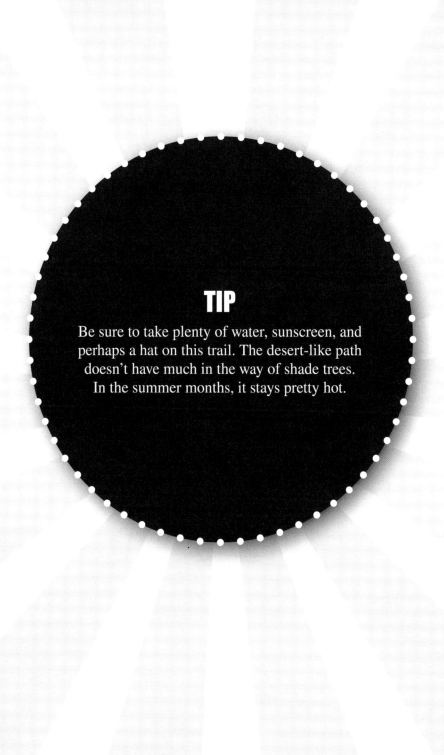

TIP

Be sure to take plenty of water, sunscreen, and perhaps a hat on this trail. The desert-like path doesn't have much in the way of shade trees. In the summer months, it stays pretty hot.

ENJOY LOADS OF FUN OR A PLACE TO RELAX
AT LORY STATE PARK

Whether you are in the mood to hike, run, rock climb, play a game of horseshoes, or simply have a picnic, Lory State Park may be just what you're looking for. Located west of Horsetooth Reservoir and only a few minutes from Old Town Fort Collins, the entrance to the park has a small museum that has information about the animals that live here and history of the area. There are some firepits and barbeque grills for those who like to cook their food on-site. Picnic tables dot the grounds and there are several larger picnic areas that can be rented for special occasions like family reunions and weddings. For the more adventurous, there are several campsites in the backcountry which can be reserved for a fee. The park also has 26 miles of trails. Open year-round, there is a fee for entrance into the park.

708 N Colorado Rd. 25G, 970-493-1623
cpw.state.co.us/placestogo/Parks/lory

ANY PLACE YOU WANT TO FROLIC

Beautiful cities have beautiful parks and Fort Collins is no exception. There are parks located all over town and whether you want to throw a Frisbee or have a picnic, you will find just the place to play. There are eight popular parks with the top three of those being City Park, Canyon Park, and Twin Silos Park. The oldest is City Park. It has a lake with a walking trail, swimming pool, and large grassy areas for public use. For more information on all the parks and their locations, visit fcgov.com/parks/.

FIND OPEN SPACE FOR ADVENTURE
AT CATHY FROMME PRAIRIE
NATURAL AREA

The Cathy Fromme Prairie Natural Area is one place where everybody can enjoy themselves and get back to nature. This paved 2.4-mile trail (one-way) has parking lots on both ends and several points of access along the winding pathway. Runners, walkers, strollers, bikers, and skateboarders all love this trail for its ease of navigation. Fossil Creek Trail gives visitors views of what the prairie was like when settlers came so long ago. It showcases the drylands and wetlands and is home to a host of animals like horny toads, songbirds, prairie dogs, coyotes, rabbits, and rattlesnakes. Near Shields Street, you will find the raptor observatory that in winter is a good place to see eagles and hawks. The trail is also a great place to watch the evening sun set behind the mountains and it hooks up to other trails so you don't have to stay on one path all day. As with Coyote Ridge, there aren't many trees here–just wide open spaces–so be sure to take sunscreen and plenty of water. The path may be paved, but when the sun is high overhead it can still get unbearably hot, so most locals prefer to go early or late in the day.

1999 Fromme Prairie Way, 970-416-2815
fcgov.com/naturalareas/finder/cathyfromme

GET BACK AND FARTHER OUT TO NATURE
AT SOAPSTONE PRAIRIE NATURAL AREA

Like other natural areas in and around Fort Collins, there are many miles of trails in the Soapstone Prairie Natural Area. However, what makes this 19,000-acre, 28-square-miles park so special isn't just its trails, but all the wildlife that lives here like jack rabbits, swift fox, pronghorn elk, burrowing owls, golden eagles, bison herds, and black-footed ferrets. It had been more than 150 years since bison roamed this prairie, but in 2015– thanks to science–a genetically pure bison bloodline from Yellowstone was reintroduced to the area. In 2014, 30 black-footed ferrets were put back into Soapstone Prairie as well.

Besides these two incredible wildlife additions, Soapstone has a popular archeological site, the Lindenmeier. This site, a National Historic Landmark, has yielded human artifacts dating back to the Ice Age. You could spend a couple days here and still have more to see, so be prepared to extend your stay.

22998 Rawhide Flats Rd., 970-416-2815
fcgov.com/naturalareas/finder/soapstone

CULTURE AND HISTORY

EXPERIENCE A LITTLE HISTORY, A WHOLE LOT OF FUN
AT JESSUP FARM ARTISAN VILLAGE

Located on a bluff just east of town, Jessup Farm Artisan Village was originally purchased as a farm around the turn of the century. Over time it changed hands and was eventually slated for development until 2011, when new owners bought it and decided to preserve it for posterity. Today, visitors of all ages will find something to enjoy and indulge their curiosity in everything from the farm animals to The Farmhouse restaurant at Jessup Farms. There are 12 businesses that operate here including Bindle Coffee and the Moore Animal Hospital. You'll also want to check out Josh & John's, the local ice cream shop, for slow-churned and gluten-free ice cream during your visit. It's a unique experience you'll treasure and tell others about for sure.

1957 Jessup Dr., 970-631-8041, jessupfarm.com

ENJOY A GOOD AFTERNOON'S ENTERTAINMENT
AT THE EXCHANGE

The Exchange is an outdoor entertainment area where people meet, greet, mingle, and enjoy the afternoons and evenings. There are 12 businesses surrounding the plaza and with The Exchange's common consumption permit, guests can enjoy beer from Crooked Stave in the common area while other guests sip wine from The Infinite Monkey. You can find tacos, ice cream, or a freshly made donut to enjoy with your favorite alcoholic drink if you so desire. But if you need to work up an appetite, no worries. You can play golf at the indoor nine-hole mini golf course, get a haircut at the barber shop, tune up or repair your bike at the self-service station, or find a book to read at the free book library. You can check out the shops or just sit in the sun and enjoy the day. Heat lamps are available when the weather starts to cool off, so put on your sweater, come on down, and enjoy everything The Exchange has to offer. You won't be sorry.

200 N College Ave., 970-267-0954
thegroupinc.com/blog/2018/12/the-exchange-old-town/

TURN BACK TIME
AT THE AVERY HOUSE

If you like history (and even if you don't), you'll enjoy stopping at the Avery House. A privately owned family home until 1962, it is now a museum, showing visitors what life was like in the early days of Fort Collins.

Its sandstone exterior is still as beautiful as it was when the home was originally built in 1879. Franklin Avery's initial $3,000 investment was a good one, but being in the banking business, he probably knew that. Today, the house belongs to the Poudre Landmarks Foundation and is listed on the National Register of Historic Places.

Open houses are held weekly on Saturdays and Sundays from 1 to 4 p.m. If you decide to take a tour of the house, well-informed docents will fill you in on its history. You will need to climb some stairs during the tour so be prepared. Large groups wanting to tour the home should make the reservation at least three weeks in advance.

328 W Mountain, 970-221-0533, poudrelandmarks.org

GET YOUR COMFY SHOES ON
FOR A HISTORIC WALKING TOUR

Before or after visiting the Avery House, you might want to explore the rest of Fort Collins on the self-guided Historic Walking Tour. You can start at Trimble Court in the heart of Old Town Fort Collins and go in any direction. You will discover an 1860s military post and learn about early residents who came to the town to raise families and seek their fortunes. From railroads to street cars, stagecoaches to horse drawn carriages, Fort Collins had it all. In addition, you'll be able to check out the Trolley Barn where the street cars are housed on this tour. The Museum of Art at the Old Post Office building and the Armstrong Hotel which dates back to 1923 are also included. In fact, there are so many sights to take in, you might want to plan on taking several days just for touring the town.

Don't worry if you get hungry on your tour. El Burrito, another historic landmark is #26 on the tour stop, offers great Mexican food in a relaxing atmosphere–something your feet might need after you've walked all over town.

You can download a Fort Collins Historic Walking Tour Guide at the Visit Fort Collins website, visitftcollins.com. So bookmark or print off your map and head on over.

1 Old Town Square Suite 107, 970-232-3840, visitftcollins.com

● ●

EXPERIENCE A WEE BIT O' IRISH
AT THE OLD TOWN IRISH PARTY

In March, everyone heads to the Old Town Square for the Old Town Irish Party. This celebration of St. Patrick's Day features something for the young and old, and you don't have to be Irish to attend. The event offers live music, circus entertainment, tattoo artists, Irish crafts, face painters for the kids, and of course, green beer. Visitors can wear green, get their hair sprayed green, or do both. How about a picture with a roaming leprechaun? No problem. Visitors will find several people dressed as the mischievous creatures lurking about here. Numerous food vendors are available and if you can't find anything you want from them, local restaurants are open to satisfy any hearty Irish appetite.

Fort Collins Town Square, 970-484-6500
downtownfortcollins.com/news/st-patricks-day/

TIP
If you are going to be here for St. Patrick's Day, you might want to sign up to get Visit Fort Collins updates for happenings around town. It's a great way to keep up on all the festival events. The website for signing up is visitftcollins.com.

LET'S HEAR IT FOR THE BOYS IN BLUE
AT THE FORT COLLINS POLICE MUSEUM

Few visitors to Fort Collins are aware of this interesting stop, but the Fort Collins Police Museum needs to be added to the touring agenda. Located in the lobby of the Fort Collins Police Department, this museum pays homage to the police presence in the city throughout its history. Designed by Denver artist and sculptor, Andy Dufford, owner of Chevo Studios, the museum incorporates sculptures and fountains to commemorate not only the men and women who serve today, but also officers who died in the line of duty.

The museum begins outside the building, 50 yards from the front door, with sculptures and a memorial garden. There is a display depicting officers and their uniforms from the 1900s to 2007 reflecting how the styles have changed over time and an exhibit showcasing the various types of weapons police officers have carried over the last hundred years.

The museum is a labor of love and a tribute to the men and women who keep the citizens of Fort Collins safe every day. Visitors will gain not only an appreciation for their law enforcers, but also for the art represented here.

2221 S Timberline Rd., 970-416-2789, fcgov.com/artspublic/gallery

WALK IN PEACE AND HARMONY
AT SHAMBHALA MOUNTAIN CENTER

Want a little peace and a lot of quiet? Visit the Shambhala Mountain Center. Located 50 miles northwest of Fort Collins, this 600-acre retreat is perfect for centering your mind, body, and soul.

While the landscape of pines, aspen trees, and grazing deer herds are enough to bring visitors solace, the heart of Shambhala is the Great Stupa of Dharmakaya. The 108-foot-tall shrine is a 20-minute hike from the parking lot up the trail through the snapping flags, but the trip is so worth it.

You can see the stupa when you first arrive, but as you walk along the trail it disappears behind a forest of trees until you cross a bridge and enter the field. Like a gem, the stupa sparkles and shimmers in the sunlight with its vivid colors of white, gold, and blue.

When you arrive, you can sit outside on one of the benches, walk around the stupa on the gravel walkway, or go inside to find a mediation spot for relaxation and contemplation. Inside, there are chairs where you can sit around the perimeter of the room or cushions on the floor in the middle. A huge golden Buddha sits in prayer behind rows of candles, inviting all who enter to stop and meditate on love, harmony, and prosperity, but most of all, peace.

There are trails through the woods and valleys you can trek while visiting. Lunch can be purchased at the Dining Hall throughout the year or you can bring your own. Workshops are held at the Center and there are accommodations for overnight stays and programmed retreats if you would like to attend. You can see the schedule and sign up on the website.

Whenever you come, for whatever reason, plan to spend at least a day in this true oasis.

151 Shambhala Way, Red Feathers, CO, 970-881-2184
shambhalamountain.org

JUMP ON THE TROLLEY
AND ENJOY *BIRNEY CAR 21*

Birney Car 21, also known as the Trolley, is operated by the Fort Collins Municipal Railway Society. On summer weekends and holidays, you can catch a ride on this piece of restored history. As early as 1907, a streetcar line began operating in Fort Collins. In 1919, the city acquired four new single-truck Birney Safety Cars. *Birney Car 21* was the first one to be used in checking the rail line for safety. When automobiles became more popular, the trolley car was retired and put on display for 27 years. Finally, it was put back into commission in the late 1980s. Today, visitors can visit the depot in City Park and hop on *Birney* for a three-mile ride around Fort Collins and learn more about its past.

1501 W Oak St., 970-224-5372, fortcollinstrolley.org

COME SEE
A VISUAL FEAST
AT THE MUSEUM OF ART FORT COLLINS

The Museum of Art Fort Collins is located in the old Fort Collins Post Office and Federal Building. Constructed in Second Renaissance Revival style in 1911, the building itself is listed on the National Register of Historic Places and is designated a Fort Collins local landmark. Visitors who love architecture will be tempted to pay as much attention to its white limestone and Alabama marble as they do to the Museum of Art itself. From fiber art to photography, visitors young and old will find something that fascinates them here. There are changing exhibits throughout the year and a host of educational classes and events. According to the museum's mission statement, their goal is "to spread the power of visual art." Tours are given by docents or visitors can take their time with self-guided tours while viewing the art on display and current exhibits.

This stop is a must-see not only for the art, but for the architectural uniqueness of the building.

201 S College Ave., 970-482-2787, moafc.org

HISTORY FLOURISHES AS LIVES END
AT GRANDVIEW CEMETERY

One of the oldest cemeteries in Fort Collins, Grandview Cemetery's 40 acres were purchased in 1887 from Thomas Connolly for $5 an acre. Sitting west of the city, Grandview is now a historical time capsule. Graves from other cemeteries were moved here as the city began to expand. Large statues and marble gravestones mark areas where Civil War, Grand Army of the Republic Post No. 7, Spanish-American War, both World Wars, and Korean War veterans have been laid to rest. Besides soldiers, visitors may find trappers, adventurers, explorers, ladies of ill-repute, and a host of other characters buried here.

The cemetery is beautifully laid out: large trees dot the landscape along with well-trimmed shrubs, beautiful patches of flowers, and lush bluegrass. History and genealogy buffs will find their research time well spent here among the many tombstones which tell the stories of the interred.

1900 W Mountain Ave., 970-221-6810, fcgov.com/cemeteries/history.php

ENJOY A CORNER OF COLOR
AT THE COLORADO STATE UNIVERSITY FLOWER TRIAL GARDEN

Purple, pink, red, blue, and gold are just a few of the perennial colors visitors will see at the Colorado State University Flower Trial Garden. Each year, around spring, CSU students and volunteers move over 1,000 different types of cultivated annual bedding plants to the outdoors to be evaluated, rated, and yes, enjoyed by plant lovers. The gardens allow students, researchers, industry representatives, and many others the opportunity to learn and evaluate through horticultural research about plants grown in the unique Rocky Mountain conditions. Visitors who are truly interested in the plants should plan to spend a couple hours just reading the names of each of them. Varieties are grouped by type and arranged in rows by colors for easy comparison.

The garden is open to the public all year round and admission is free. While summer is the time to see the most beautiful flower displays, pansy lovers will appreciate the fall when these flowers are showcased. Be sure to take a camera and have a pen and paper handy to jot down and record your favorites.

970-491-0108, flowertrials.colostate.edu/index.php

THINGS ARE JUST PEACHY
AT THE FORT COLLINS PEACH FESTIVAL

In August, everyone comes together in Civic Center Park in downtown Fort Collins for the Fort Collins Peach Festival. The Festival has grown every year since it started in 2011. Organizers believe that is because everyone loves peaches. The event kicks off with a 5K race, a peach pancake breakfast, and then a gathering to celebrate the fuzzy fruit for the rest of the day with vendors and samples. The festival hosts live music, and there is a Kids Zone so the young ones can work off some of that sugar from the peach cobbler they ate for lunch. Guests will find everything from peach cobbler to peach beer to indulge in on-site, but there's a lot more peachiness happening here. Palisade peaches are available for purchase as well as peach margaritas, peach ice cream, crepes with peaches, and peach jellies, jams, and syrups. Artwork, pottery, and specialty clothing vendors also get in on the fun by showcasing their wares between activities and events.

Downtown Fort Collins, fortcollinspeachfestival.com

EXPERIENCE A PIECE OF HISTORY
AT THE MASONIC TEMPLE

While this building is not open to the public per se, if they are interested, visitors might be able to arrange a special tour. Construction of the Classical Revival–style Masonic Temple building was begun in 1925 when the cornerstone was laid and was completed in 1927. This cream-colored brick building with its six Tuscan columns is meant to remind visitors of other Masonic Temples around the world.

Designed by William H. Bowman, the building has held dances, offices, a library, and of course, Masons meetings. Currently, there is a main hall lined with pictures of those involved with the Fort Collins Masons throughout the years, and the building also houses offices, meeting rooms, and a small museum. If you aren't fortunate enough to get a tour inside, drive by to take a picture of the outside. After all, it has been added to the Colorado Register of Historic Places.

225 W Oak St., 970-884-3468, frontnet.com/temple/

LOOK FOR THE SOUP CAN
IN FRONT OF THE GREGORY ALLICAR MUSEUM OF ART

People may not know that Fort Collins has an art museum to rival others across the country. Located in the Colorado University Center for the Arts on the southeast corner of the campus, the Gregory Allicar Museum of Art is free and open to the public. It has seven galleries within its 10,000-square-foot interior and there are 4,000 gallery objects on display. Items include over 1,500 African artifacts including carvings, metal work, ceramics, beadwork, contemporary art, screen prints, and photography. There are works by European Old Masters from the Italian Renaissance and French Baroque periods as well as works from pop artist Andy Warhol. An easy way to spot the location of the museum is to look for the 10-foot-tall *Campbell's Tomato Soup Can* sitting right outside the museum's front door. Before going in, stop and take a look at the sculpture to see where Warhol signed it when he visited the art building on September 1, 1981.

1400 Remington, 970-491-1989, artmuseum.colostate.edu

GREGORY ALLICAR MUSEUM OF ART

COLORADO STATE UNIVERSITY

artmuseum.colostate.edu

1400

Photo courtesy of the Gregory Allicar
Museum of Art

GET SOME CULTURE
AT THE LINCOLN CENTER

Culture and the arts are alive and well in Fort Collins. If you like visual art look no further than The Art Gallery housed in The Lincoln Center which features changing art exhibits from juried competitions, national artists, and sometimes even traveling art shows. If you want to see a show, The Lincoln Center has two performing art areas: an over 1,100-seat performance hall and a 220-seat theatre. Together they accommodate professional theatre shows, dance performances, musical concerts, and more. Some of the most popular shows that have been performed here are *The Nutcracker, The Color Purple*, and *Jersey Boys*. The Center is also a multi-purpose event center hosting trade shows, conferences, conventions, and even weddings in their ballrooms, interior locations, and their outdoor areas like the outdoor sculpture garden. You don't have to spring for a show to visit The Lincoln Center; just set aside some time to meander through the gardens or see the latest installations at The Art Gallery.

417 W Magnolia, 970-221-6733, lctix.com

BUTTERFLIES GALORE AND MORE
AT THE BUTTERFLY HOUSE

The Butterfly House, located on the grounds of The Gardens on Spring Creek, is sanctuary to hundreds of butterflies and moths like Monarchs and Painted Ladies in their own simulated tropical environment. The colorful insects fly freely here and while they most commonly land on some of the hundreds of varieties of plants available for viewing in the sanctuary, they may just be curious enough to land on you as well. There is a 2,200-square-foot wall of plants where the moths and butterflies prefer to light, but the unique thing about this house is the chrysalis window. You can watch butterflies emerge from their chrysalises behind the glass and that in itself is worth the visit. This is your chance to get a close-up look at the environment these winged-creatures live in, but also to learn about their life cycle through the caterpillar display.

2145 Centre Ave., 970-416-2486, fcgov.com/gardens/butterfly-house

SEE BOTANICAL BEAUTY AT ITS BEST
AT THE GARDENS ON SPRING CREEK

If you like plants–any kind of plants–from roses to cacti, a must-visit is The Gardens on Spring Creek. There are 16 different gardens located on 18 acres ranging from the Rock Garden and the Garden of Eatin' to the Theme Gardens which feature five specialty plots like the Rose and Moon Gardens. The themed plantings range in size from a 350-foot boulevard strip to the two-acre Great Lawn. In these gardens, you will learn not only how to grow plants, but also how to cook with and take care of different herbs and vegetables while visiting and enjoying nature at its finest. The Spring Creek curators didn't leave the kids out of this educational experience. The Children's Garden comprises all the other gardens but on a smaller scale. There are many interactive things for children and their parents to do. For sure, kids will want to visit the Dr. Seuss Playhouse and Sandpit, Miniature Train Garden, and Animal Footprint Path. From backyard landscaping ideas to growing your own food, both professional and novice botanists can learn something new and fascinating here. Bring a lunch and plan to spend all day.

2145 Centre Ave., 970-416-2486, fcgov.com/gardens

TIP

Numerous events take place here year-round.
The largest and most well-attended of these is
the Garden of Lights. Every December during
the Christmas holiday season, the gardens are
decorated in lights and curators invite the public
in to experience the magic.

LIGHT UP THE HOLIDAY
AT THE DOWNTOWN CHRISTMAS LIGHTING CEREMONY

When the holiday season rolls around, Fort Collins kicks off the celebration with the Downtown Christmas Lighting Ceremony. Thousands of lights illuminate the alleyways, sidewalks, street tops, storefronts, and Old Town trees along College Avenue and down LaPorte Avenue and Walnut. Besides strolling down the streets enjoying the beauty, you can sip hot chocolate, enjoy a holiday meal at one of the restaurants, or shop at one of the local stores for Christmas gifts (or something for yourself). Don't worry if you can't make it on Christmas Day, you'll have plenty of time to see the lights: they stay lit from November 1 to February 14th.

Downtown Fort Collins, 970-221-6760, fcgov.com

TIP

If you're in town around the holidays be sure to check out the Garden of Lights at the Gardens on Spring Creek. Stroll through a winter wonderland and enjoy the magic of the season. (2145 Centre Ave., 970-416-2486)

ART IS TRULY EVERYWHERE
AT THE DOWNTOWN PUBLIC ART TOUR

Starting at the corner of Laporte Avenue and Mason Street, art lovers are in for quite an experience if they follow the self-guided Downtown Public Art Tour. From paver inlays on the street corners to bronze sculptures of fanciful dancers throughout the Downtown area, local artists are supported and represented. In the Civic Center Parking Garage there is a huge, brightly colored modern mural designed by muralist and children's book illustrator, Rafael Lopez, painted by volunteers and sponsored by the Poudre Valley Public Library District. All over town you will find Water Quality Boxes designed to feature art as well as art panels titled *Sustainable Garden*, cabinet murals, and colorful *Pianos About Town*. These are designed to showcase art and make the downtown area a place that truly shines. You can download your own art tour map by visiting fcgov.com/artspublic.

281 N College Ave., 970-221-6760, fcgov.com/artspublic

GO GLOBAL
ALL IN ONE SPACE
AT THE GLOBAL VILLAGE
MUSEUM OF ART

Visitors who like to check out international culture will not want to miss the Global Village Museum of Arts. It is the only museum in Colorado that focuses on international collections and is home to folk art, fine art, and artifacts of all kinds donated by local collectors and founding members. Several galleries are housed here including the Mundoville Gallery (International Folk Art in Miniature) and the Village Arts Gallery itself. Throughout the year there are rotating exhibits in the Main Gallery and Hall Gallery. The most popular displays have included *China's Imperial Treasures Art and Artifacts*; *Egypt: Gift of the Nile*; and the *Russian Retrospective* to name only three of the more impressive exhibits.

Along with curating exhibits, the Global Village Museum hosts several events throughout the year. The Art Walk is held the first Friday of each month and admission is free on those evenings. There are a total of 17 summer programs which coincide with the Main Galley Exhibit and the Annual Fundraising Gala. Check the website to learn more about the Museum and see all the happenings.

200 W Mountain Ave., #C, 970-221-4600, globalvillagemuseum.org

● ●

HAVE A FURILICIOUS GOOD TIME
AT TOUR DE CORGI

What's cuter than a short-legged bundle of fur? A short-legged bundle of fur in a costume. Every year in September, Welsh corgi lovers meet up in Fort Collins for their annual event, the Tour de Corgi. There's the usual meet and greet, but the main event is the parade and costume contest. Not only do the corgis wear costumes, but so do their owners. Once everybody gets dressed up it's time to walk in front of the judges and then strut their stuff through Old Town Fort Collins. The public is invited to come out because, besides the corgi events, there are other dog-related vendor booths. Everybody has a good time and some are lucky enough to get a wet, slobbery kiss from their favorite pooch. Visit their website to get exact dates.

Civic Center Park, tourdecorgi.org

LET IT GO
AT THE FORT COLLINS
WATER LANTERN FESTIVAL

"Total Magic" is how this event has been described. People of all ages from different cultures and backgrounds come together to dream a little, remember, and hope. The Fort Collins Water Lantern Festival is held in September at Boyd Lake State Park.

When you arrive you will receive a paper lantern. You can write a letter to a loved one, put down your dreams or goals, or simply draw pictures on the four sides. It's your lantern and it can be a good meditation exercise. Some people spend months prior to the event thinking about how they want to decorate their lanterns. You don't have to be an artist: You just have to "be."

While it is an all-day event with music, food, and drink, the magic happens at night when all the lanterns are launched into the water. Everyone grows quiet. Some people cry, others cheer. It is a beautiful experience both personally and collectively. Make time for this. You won't regret it.

Boyd Lake State Park, waterlanternfestival.com

EXPERIENCE A FARM TOUR OF A DIFFERENT FLAVOR
AT MORNING FRESH DAIRY

If you like Noosa Yoghurt, you might want to check out the dairy farm that supplies the milk for this Aussie-inspired treat. Morning Fresh Dairy even shares the same property with the yoghurt plant, which is just outside Fort Collins. This farm is a fifth-generation, family-owned business and has been in operation since 1894, so as you can imagine they know how to raise their cows to turn out the best milk possible. At Morning Fresh you'll learn about farming, meet the cows, and see the lovely countryside the cows call home. The tours start and stop at the Howling Cow Café and last for about an hour and a half. This is a free walking tour so wear comfy shoes. After you have learned all about the farm, you can enjoy samples of the milk and Noosa Yoghurt or purchase sandwiches, sweet snacks, or even an espresso at the Café.

5821 W County Rd. 54 E, 970-482-5789, morningfreshdairy.com

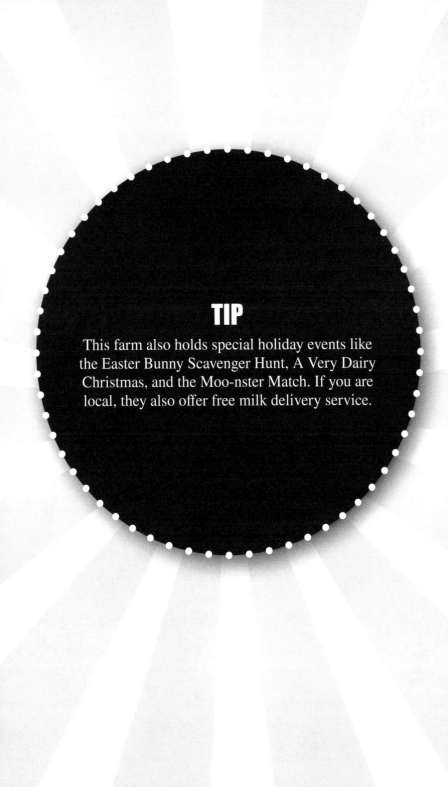

TIP

This farm also holds special holiday events like the Easter Bunny Scavenger Hunt, A Very Dairy Christmas, and the Moo-nster Match. If you are local, they also offer free milk delivery service.

Photo courtesy of Nuance Chocolate

SHOPPING AND FASHION

GET YOUR TORCHES ON
AT GLASS AND FIRE

With 60 years collective experience, Ron Murphy and his sons invite you to come in to Glass and Fire in Fort Collins to witness how they use fire to turn glass into works of art. While there are several glass images of Colorado wildlife here, the Murphys are currently focused on different kinds of ocean life like sea turtles, octopuses, and fish made into realistic glass sculptures or pendants. You might be able to buy their pieces at other stores, but at the studio you can watch the artwork being made.

1909 Timberline Lane, 970-402-3280, glassnfire.com

TIP

Glass and Fire also offers glass-blowing classes for beginners. Check out their website to learn about dates and times.

EXPLORE THE SPICE OF IT
AT OLD TOWN SPICE SHOP

If you love to cook (or even if you don't) a visit to the Old Town Spice Shop is a unique shopping experience. A family-owned business, the Godbey family imports spices from all over the world directly from their countries of origin, fresh-grinds them, and not only sells the individual spices, but makes their own blends.

The minute you step inside the door you will experience the wonderful aromas of cinnamon, peppermint, or maybe cardamom, depending on what the family is grinding that day. Add the friendly atmosphere with knowledgeable staff who can answer any questions you might have or point you in the direction of a particular spice and you know this is a place you will visit again.

Besides their house blends like Devil's Backbone, Beach House Blend, and Mishawaka Falls, Old Town Spice Shop has flavored salts and sugars as well as cocoas and loose-leaf teas.

130 S College Ave. A, 970-493-7206, thespicehouse.com

DO THE MOU
AT MOUCO CHEESE

While you can find this soft-ripened cheese in stores, MouCo Cheese is manufactured and sold in Fort Collins. This cheese company has been here since 2001. In 2019, two of their cheeses, MouCo Ashley and MouCo ColoRouge each won a Bronze Medal at the World Cheese Championship in Italy.

MouCo Cheese has six different cheeses made from local ingredients, so you know these cheeses are fresh. Their most popular item is the Cheddar Cheese Curds and most customers want them right when they come out of the cheese vat. When curds are being made MouCo lets interested patrons know via text.

Customers can visit the facility to buy curds and other cheeses or take a tour. Tours are held Tuesday and Wednesday mornings by appointment only. If you love cheese, you gotta go.

1401 Duff Dr., #300, 970-498-0107, mouco.com

TAKE A WALK DOWN MEMORY LANE
AT A & J ANTIQUE MALL

If you like vintage pieces or are just looking for a blast from your past, stop into A & J Antique Mall. With over 110 dealers, this 13,000-square-foot small antique mall will either take you back to your childhood or teleport you to another time.

Each booth holds a different treasure. You can browse through the books, check out the household goods like the crank-handle handheld mixers or inspect the antique jewelry. A customer once found an eighteenth-century brooch in perfect condition here. Children and grandchildren love to visit this store. The owners are always willing to answer questions and spend a little extra time with the inquisitive, especially young people who want to know things like what is a spittoon and how was it used?

This mall has everything from toys to table toppers like doilies. So if you're looking for something specific or just want to relive your childhood, stop by. Plan to spend several hours here: this is a place you don't want to rush through.

6012 S College Ave., 970-226-6070, ajantiquemall.com

DISCOVER THE PAST
AT ANTIQUE ROW

If you can't find what you're looking for at A&J's, don't despair. There are six other antique stores set along the same street on Antique Row. Each one comes with its own set of unique items. North Fork Antiques (6004 S College Ave., 970-377-1522) has a lot of decorating ideas. You will find different ways to repurpose old furniture or restore it to its original condition. Vintage Marketplace (6520 S College Ave., 970-672-8048) has everything…well…vintage from horseshoes and butcher-block tables to metal television trays and large washtubs. We found things there that my grandma used to have and use like hand-cranked blenders, butter churns, and cast-iron skillets. Fort Collins Flea Market (6200 S College Ave., 970-223-6502) and Foothills Flea Market & Antiques (6300 S College Ave., 970-223-9069) has things you didn't know you needed until you saw them. For instance, if you need a part for an older model vacuum cleaner, you might find it here. Jarvey's Treasures (6108 S College Ave., 970-217-2693) has vintage signs aplenty and old toys that are collectibles. All you need is time and the thrill of the hunt.

FIND SOLID TO THE CORE
AT WOODLEY'S FINE FURNITURE

Woodley's Fine Furniture makes furniture shopping fun and easy. From office furniture to bedroom decor and everything in between, this store has not only just what you are looking for but also things you didn't even know you were interested in. Even if you are not looking to buy, go into this Colorado-based store for decorating ideas. Woodley's Fine Furniture is an institution in Fort Collins and the surrounding area for its well-designed solid wood furniture. Their show room is spacious and inviting and the smell of wood and leather is a treat for the senses. While the showroom is spectacular, don't forget to check out the sale items in the warehouse at the back of the store.

The people here are friendly and always willing to answer questions. Don't worry about bringing a truck: Woodley's delivers.

501 S College Ave., 970-282-7228, woodleys.com

GET YOUR ARTIST ON
AT BOARD AND BRUSH

If you want to spend an evening or a whole weekend doing something a little different, you need to visit Board and Brush. This family-oriented business is just the place for you to indulge your creative curiosity. Since the projects here are personalized signs or hangings made of wood, think hammer, drill, and paint brush.

When you sign up for a workshop or drop by on the first Friday of a given month, you'll learn how to work with raw materials, sand and stain your project, and distress or wax wood to achieve the desired effect so you can leave with a work of art you created and will want to display. You don't have to be Van Gogh or Picasso: transferrable artwork and inspiring phrases are available for use on your masterpiece. With over 400-plus options, even the pickiest artist will find something endearing and board-worthy.

244 N College Ave., Suite 115, 970-213-1575, boardandbrush.com

THE NEAT PLACE TO KNIT
IS AT MY SISTER KNITS

Take a stroll down a rock walk through an English-style garden to the inviting brick carriage house and enter a knitting- and crochet-lover's paradise. When Julie Lukasen opened her shop, My Sister Knits, in 2004, she had no idea she would have guests visiting from all over the world.

Male or female, beginner or advanced, knitter or crochet enthusiast, all of the store's patrons revel in the colors, textures, and patterns of the many different types of fibers found here. From Hedgehog Fibers and Shibui Knits to Tuku Wool and Forbidden Fibers, once you walk through the yellow door, you are surrounded by vibrant colors and soft fiber, fabric, and yarn. Don't hesitate to reach out to feel the yarns and threads or ask about accessories and classes. Come for the fibers but stay to enjoy all the other perks this cottage has to offer.

1408 W Mountain Ave., 970-407-1461, mysisterknits.com

NEED KITCHEN STUFF?
FIND IT AT THE CUPBOARD

If you love to cook and kitchen gadgets are your thing, The Cupboard is the place for you. With over 20,000 items–all kitchen related–this store has a plethora of things for chefs and chef want-to-bes like dinnerware, cutlery, tea, candy, pottery, and more.

The Cupboard has been a staple in Fort Collins for more than 45 years since owner Carey Hewitt started the business in 1972 as an alternative to teaching math. The store is located in a building dating from the early 1900s, so visitors can experience the homelike atmosphere of brick walls and squeaking wood floors.

This store offers several events throughout the year and some of the more popular activities include their charity knife-sharpening event, weekend demonstrations, and food samplings.

152 S College Ave., 970-493-8585, thecupboard.net

FIND THE TRUE MEANING OF A PLANT LOVERS PARADISE
AT THE FORT COLLINS NURSERY

The Fort Collins Nursery began as a vegetable farm back in 1932. That little plot of ground has grown into 17,000 square feet of retail space that includes an indoor greenhouse and garden shop, three acres of outdoor retail, and then six more acres of nursery where plants are grown to sell. All kinds of plants can be found here including trees, shrubs, vegetables, house plants, and flowers. The Nursery also carries any tool you might need for the garden along with books to tell you how to use those tools for the plants you want to grow.

People drive here from all over to shop at the Nursery. One Wyoming customer said, "I've been coming to this nursery since I was two. It's the only place I feel confident to get the plants I like to grow." This is definitely a place where you will want to spend some time and if you have a question, the Nursery professionals will have just the answers you need.

2121 Mulberry St., 970-482-1984, fortcollinsnursery.com

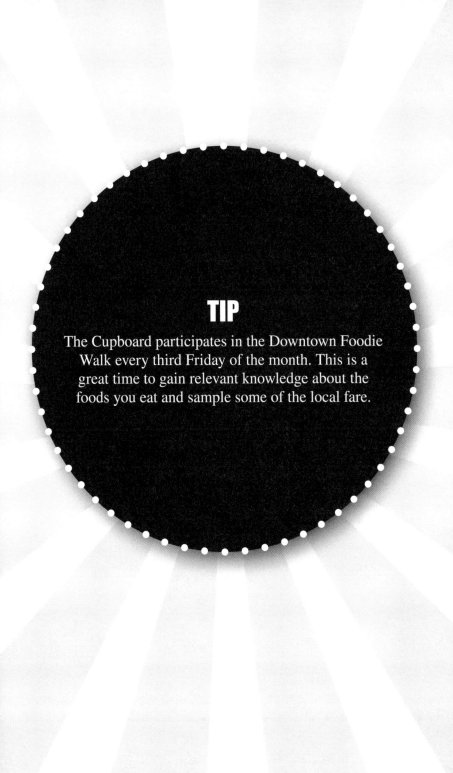

TIP

The Cupboard participates in the Downtown Foodie Walk every third Friday of the month. This is a great time to gain relevant knowledge about the foods you eat and sample some of the local fare.

GET TOTALLY OUT OF CONTROL
AT NUANCE CHOCOLATE

Lovers of chocolate owe it to themselves to visit Nuance Chocolate. The owners started their business after a vacation to Costa Rica where what started as a hobby went out of control. Once they learned the process of taking the cacao bean to delicious chocolate treats, they decided they wanted to bring their new-found passion to Colorado, so they did.

Unlike chocolatiers who buy chocolate to make their treats, Nuance chocolate-makers develop chocolate from scratch. They start with the raw cacao beans, then roast, crack, winnow, grind, and temper them to follow all the steps that go into chocolate-making right in Old Town Fort Collins.

As a result, they turn out some of the best truffles, hot drinks, and bean-to-bar chocolate candy in the world. Nuance Chocolate hosts after-hours educational events so would-be chocolatiers can learn the art and science of chocolate, too. Definitely a must-stop when visiting Fort Collins.

214 Pine St., 970-484-2330, nuancechocolate.com

FEED YOUR BURNING DESIRE TO READ
AT OLD FIREHOUSE BOOKS

If you like old books, new books, borrowed books, or blue books, you need to check out Old Firehouse Books. Northern Colorado's largest independent bookstore and one of its last, Old Firehouse has books of all genres for readers of all ages. The bookstore opened in 1980, then moved into the old historic firehouse in 2009 and took its name in homage to the location. While there is a lot that is unique about this bookstore, probably the most interesting thing is that used books sit right alongside new books on the shelves. Of course, the used books are marked as such and the ratio of new to used is 70 to 30 percent, respectively. The stores carries no hardcover books–everything is paperback. There is seating throughout the store for those who want to sample the wares while they browse. You might also want to check out events that bring in local and national authors, Story Time for children held every Tuesday morning, and the themed book clubs hosted at the store. There are four book clubs that meet in the back room every month, including lovers of graphic novels, citizens who want to be politically informed, and armchair detectives who devour mysteries. The store is open to hosting other clubs if one of these doesn't meet your needs. The founder of the bookstore wanted it to be fun. Visit and judge for yourself.

232 Walnut St., 970-484-7898, oldfirehousebooks.com

ANY TIME IS THE RIGHT TIME FOR TEA
AT HAPPY LUCKY'S TEAHOUSE

After stopping at Old Firehouse Books, pop in next door to Happy Lucky's Teahouse. The name blends their two mottos: "Nourish Your Happy," and "Be Your Lucky." The goal of Happy Lucky's was to create a community atmosphere in a place where people could go, sit down with a friend, and enjoy a good cup of tea. From the minute you walk into this 100-year-old building, you can smell the comforting aroma of tea. They have over 200 loose leaf teas to choose from (the largest selection in the state of Colorado). If that doesn't get your attention, experience "the Great Wall of Tea," made up of 30 to 35 percent proprietary blends made just for Lucky's. You can get hot tea, cold tea, and local Kombucha on-tap to go or to stay. There is enough indoor and outside seating for 28 people. Leafsters are there to answer any questions you may have and even to help you blend something special for yourself. You will also find a fine array of teapots, tea canisters, and everything tea in between.

236 Walnut St., 970-689-3417, happyluckys.com

DISCOVER YOUR OWN NATURE'S GUIDE TO HEALTH AND WELLNESS
AT GOLDEN POPPY HERBAL APOTHECARY

If you are looking to switch from commercial body products to natural ones, you owe it to yourself to visit the Golden Poppy Herbal Apothecary. Some of their favorite customers are the ones who seek natural solutions. Golden Poppy offers over 100 different herbs and their own line of essential oils. Everything in this 1,700-square-foot location is handmade in the store and is natural and organic. Customers can get a consultation and custom formulations here for everything from sleeping to digestive issues. On the shelves you can find aromatherapy products, herbal tea blends, body sprays, soaps, and lotions. Everybody who works here is trained in aromatherapy or herbology. So, if you are looking for healthy alternatives to products with harmful chemicals or you just need something a little different, come here.

223 N College Ave., 970-682-4373, goldenpoppyherbs.com

GET YOUR BLING ON
AT ROCKY MOUNTAIN GOLDWORKS

For handmade and one-of-a-kind jewelry visit Rocky Mountain Goldworks in Old Town Fort Collins. Combining over 40 years of experience with modern CAD technology, the jewelers here can translate your ideas and designs into stunning pieces of art for you to wear. If you want to get "hands-on" with your own designs, you can do that here too. You can pour your own metal and be the first to touch your cast pieces. Custom pieces take about six to eight weeks to complete.

Designs for earrings, necklaces, bracelets, and rings can be made up or purchased on-site in gold and silver, but they must send out any designs which incorporate platinum. Besides making jewelry, at Goldworks you can also have your favorite sentimental or heirloom pieces repaired. If you're looking for a piece of jewelry that is uniquely yours or you need something fixed, be sure to stop in at Rocky Mountain Goldworks.

200 N College Ave., 970-267-0954, goldworks.com

BECOME A LITTLE LOOPY
AT LOOPY EWE

In 2006, Sheri Berger took her daughter to a local craft store in the hopes of getting her hooked on a hobby. Little did she know, 14 years later, that Berger herself would own the Loopy Ewe, a craft shop synonymous with yarn for knitters and those who crochet. Anyone who has ever worked with yarn has probably ordered something from Sheri Berger. She carries everything from luxury fibers to independently or commercially dyed yarns and mail order is a big part of the business. However, if you're in Fort Collins, you'll want to stop in and pick up a pattern and some yarn in person. You'll find knitting needles, crochet hooks, yarns, patterns, and everything you will need to get your project underway and through to completion. Berger's goal was to build a sense of community and she has succeeded. This is evident in the care and attention she and her staff give to customers and the connection she has made with people throughout the years. Patrons are welcome to sit on the red couches, stay awhile, and see samples of all the lovely projects they can make.

4856 Innovation Dr., Suite A, 888-527-9181, theloopyewe.com

SHOP FOR ADVENTURE
AT AKINZ

Living the adventurous life is what Akinz is all about. And if you are living it, you should have clothes that show it. From T-shirts and tank tops to hats and now masks, you will find whatever you are looking for at this store.

Suzanne Akin started her company in Houston, Texas in 2005. Today, the Fort Collins location is the In-house Production location for all the other stores. With their wings logo and "Find Your Wings" motto, this store encourages your adventurous soul whether you snowboard, ski, bike, or hike. Akinz is definitely the place to go to get your adventure gear.

15 Old Town Square #132, 970-682-1750, akinz.com

IT'S MORE
THAN THE SALT
AT SAVORY SPICE SHOP

Is your food tasting a little bland lately? Not to worry; the Savory Spice Shop is here to rescue your recipes and tickle your taste buds back to life. With over 450 spice options–300 straight spices and 150 combinations–you are sure to find seasonings that will enhance the flavor of everything you eat. The herbs, spices, and sauces are brought in from all over the world and represent some of the freshest flavors available today. The five cinnamon spices are best sellers here as well as the taco seasonings. Customers who must eliminate salt from their diets love this store for its salt-free and limited salt combinations. Everything in the store is made from the best ingredients. Don't just be a good cook; let Savory Spice make you a great one.

123 N College Ave., 970-682-2971, savoryspiceshop.com

SHOP AND STAY AWHILE
AT NATURE'S OWN

Across from the Old Fort Collins Town Square is Nature's Own. Part museum, part store, this shop has something for everyone. In the front of the store, you will find fossils and rocks–small, medium, and large. As one customer said, "No matter what stone I need, they have it here." There are geodes that can be cracked open right on the premises if you find one that is still intact. The staff is knowledgeable in all things "rock," so if you have questions, don't hesitate to ask. Besides impressive stones, they have crystals, minerals, stone chess sets, and meteorite specimens. The merchandise includes jewelry, books, kits, rugs, rock magnets, T-shirts, and even stuffed animals. There is so much to see; plan to spend the whole morning or afternoon browsing the shelves. Be sure to go all the way to the back—you might find some real gems in the clearance section there.

201 Linden St., #101, 970-484-9701, naturesown.com

LOVE THE SPECIALTY
AT THE WELSH RABBIT CHEESE SHOP

From the sign to the little shop inside, The Welsh Rabbit Cheese Shop will grab your heart and your palate the minute you step through the door. This quaint little cheese shop has an impressive selection of over 50 cheeses at any given time that come from all over the world, ranging from Cotswold English cheese to Idiazabal from Spain. Cheese connoisseurs will be impressed by the selection. The shop also has specialty crackers and chocolates, fruit preserves, and mustards, so when you leave you will be fully stocked. You can also get cheese knives and hand-crafted cutting boards here. This shop also carries French baguettes and Peppadew and Peruvian Sweety Drop Peppers. It's a nice little place to drop into, ask questions about cheeses, and find just the thing you need to meet your entertaining needs.

216 Pine St., 970-443-4027, thewelshrabbit.com

TIP

If you enjoyed the cheese shop, you might want to pop into The Welsh Rabbit Bistro right around the corner. Here you'll find charcuterie plates, cheeses from the cheese shop, and different kinds of meat like smoked duck, prosciutto, and salami. Sit down to enjoy or take it to go.

AVOID HARD KNOCKS
AT OTTERBOX

You might know Otterbox as the company that makes the hard, durable phone cases that you buy to protect your phone against damage when you drop it, but they are so much more. Starting in 1998, the Otterbox mission has been to make products that allow customers to do more of what they want to do—live life to its fullest. With their commitment to build products a step above the usual fare, this company has cultivated a brand people know they can trust.

At the Otter Shop in old downtown Fort Collins, you can browse all their current products from phone cases and coolers to duffle bags, mugs, growlers, and more. One customer suggested the products at the Otter Shop might just be indestructible, so you owe it to yourself and your adventures to get a few of these products for yourself.

151 W Mountain Ave., 970-825-5650, otterbox.com

THINGS ARE BETTER HERE
AT FORT COLLINS OLD TOWN SQUARE

A great place to sit down, enjoy one of the local brews, and decide where to go next is Fort Collins Old Town Square. Amid the trees and plants here, you'll find cooling fountains and restful places to sit and ponder. Look around: you will see places to grab a quick meal or shops to visit within walking distance in all directions. Once you order, you can sit outside and enjoy your meal in the sunshine. There are art galleries here and many of the historic tours pass through this area. Throughout the year, many different events are held in the Old Town Square from concerts to art festivals. This popular gathering place is the pulse of the city and welcomes all visitors to enjoy the beauty and different shopping, dining, and entertainment experiences offered here. When visiting Fort Collins, this is one area of town you don't want to miss.

Downtown Old Fort Collins, 970-232-3840
visitfortcollins.com/maps-info/neighborhoods/old-town/

FIND A LITTLE BIT OF THIS, A WHOLE LOT OF THAT
AT CURIOSITIES

At first glance, you may think this shop is just your average gift shop but you will find that in Curiosities first impressions can be deceiving. Step inside and you will discover an eclectic and unique specialty store. Every nook and cranny are packed with something fun and spectacular. Chimes, disco balls, and Tiffany-inspired lamps hang from the ceiling. There are coffee mugs, wine glasses, water bottles, and even knee-high socks with phrases knitted into their patterns that will suit any personality from grumpy or whimsical to even the self-professed people haters of the world. No matter which animal species you are fond of, this shop has the bag, billfold, or hat to indulge your fancy. From sloths to kitties, they have you covered. As you wander through the store, you'll find kitchen towels, onesies, metal lunch boxes, and greeting cards. Don't just shop the front of the store. All the way in the back is where they keep the journals, dinosaurs, gnomes, incense, and all your super-hero items. Plan to spend a lot of time here because just when you think you've seen it all, you will turn around and find something you missed. Every nook and cranny are packed with something fun and spectacular.

242 Walnut St., 970-495-0684, curiositiesfoco.com

● ●

DISCOVER ALL THINGS FERMENTED
AT TURTLE MOUNTAIN FERMENTERY

If you like sweet tea, but have never tried Kombucha, you're missing out. These drinks are not only sweet tasting but are healthy for you as well because they contain probiotics that support your immune and digestive systems to name one of the many health benefits. When sisters Hannah and Natalie DiSanto started the business in 2014, they frequented the farmers markets of Northern Colorado. Today, Turtle Mountain Fermentery has its own taproom where guests can experience Kombucha Flights, fermented veggie boards, and hot tea by the cup or pot. Besides the seven rotating Kombucha flavors like Lavender Grape, Apple Pie, Yerba Mate, Ambrosia, Ginger, and Rose Petal, the taproom also sells Kimchi and packaged herbal teas and will fill your growler. A lot of people come to Fort Collins for the beer, but don't miss stopping here and trying Kombucha. You might find you have a new favorite drink.

513 N Link Lane, Unit C, 720-446-6170, turtlemountainfermentery.com

GET IT FRESH FROM THE START
AT ROCKY MOUNTAIN OIL COMPANY

If you like fresh or infused olive oil or vinegars from balsamic to raspberry, you will want to stop in at the Rocky Mountain Oil Company. From the minute you step off the street onto the wooden floor, you'll know you have found another Fort Collins treasure. Lined along the walls and in the center on special racks are huge vats of olive oils and vinegars. Some are pre-bottled or you can bottle your own. The friendly staff will answer any questions you may have if you're looking for something in particular and offer helpful suggestions if you are not sure what you want. Bottles are available for purchase in three different sizes so you can leave with one large bottle of something you love and a few smaller bottles of something to try. Whatever you decide to buy here, you will want to come back for more.

123 N College Ave. Suite 170, 970-484-8101, rockymountainoils.com

TIP

For an all-natural sorbet, purchase one of their fruit vinegars. Buy frozen fruit to match your vinegar like raspberries or peaches. In a blender, put two cups of frozen fruit, two tablespoons of fruit vinegar, and water as needed to get the consistency you would like. Blend.

SOME LIKE IT HOT
AT ROBERTO'S SALSA AND SAUCES

Made with the freshest ingredients like vine-ripened tomatoes, onions, and cilantro, Roberto's Salsa and Sauces are true favorites up and down the Front Range. Customers have said it is their favorite place to buy spicy dipping and cooking sauces. These products first became popular when they were served at Roberto's restaurant. The restaurant is now closed, but the salsa and sauces continue to be made and sold at Roberto's shop. From pineapple to extra hot habanero salsa, you can find it all on the shelves of this store. You'll want to drop in, sample the many flavors, and find some new favorites.

2121 S College Ave., 970-224-3006, robertos-salsa.com

RELEASE YOUR INNER CHILD
AT CLOTHES PONY & DANDELION TOYS

A fun place to shop with and for kids is Clothes Pony & Dandelion Toys. When you first look in the windows, it looks like the store only sells children's clothes, but there is much more inside. While clothes cover a big section of the store, there is also a huge selection of eclectic toys that will take you down memory lane whether you have children or are expecting them. There are many things to see and touch here from plain to shiny hula hoops and little wooden train sets to building blocks and stuffed animals. If your little one is into crafts or you want to get him or her started in one, there are many kids' craft kits here. Puzzles, books, science kits, and paint sets can also be found on the shelves. Moms and dads as well as grandpas and grandmas always find something at Clothes Pony & Dandelion Toys to keep the little ones busy and dressed to the nines.

111 N College Ave., 970-224-2866, clothespony.com

SPREAD BEAUTY
AT BLOOM FLOWER MARKET

When Cindy Gilbert started Bloom Flower Market some years ago, she intended to sell flowers from a cart she peddled around town. That concept quickly changed when her business started to grow. Today, her shop is somewhat hidden, located as it is up the street from The Still Whiskey Steaks in the alley next to the LaPorte Parking Garage. People who find her, though, are glad they did because Gilbert gets to know her customers in the warm, cozy, friendly environment of her shop.

Cindy Gilbert likes to say she sells flower-related items such as fresh flowers, plants, succulents, vases, small bags of organic flower "tea" cards made by a local artist, floral cards, and select lip balms and hand salves. Visiting Bloom's is like stepping into a world of serenity, which is why many customers return not only in person but through monthly and bimonthly subscription services. Gilbert invites you into her world, one you'll be glad you visited.

155 N College Ave., Suite 130, 970-893-2907, flowershopfortcollins.com

A FEW MORE EVENTS YOU MIGHT WANT TO CHECK OUT

Colorado Brewers' Festival
Downtown Fort Collins, 970-484-6500
downtownfortcollins.com

Fourth of July Celebration
Downtown Fort Collins, 970-221-6875, fcgov.com

Old Town Zombie Fest
Old Town, downtownfortcolllins.com

Photo courtesy of Unsplash

SUGGESTED
ITINERARIES

DATE NIGHT

NATURAL BEAUTY

HISTORY AWAITS

· ·

A FRIGHTENING GOOD TIME

FOR THE YOUNG 'UNS

YOUR OWN FOODIE TOUR

• •

GET YOUR ZEN ON

ACTIVITIES
BY SEASON

SPRING

You'll Find the Right Stuff at The Emporium: An American Brasserie, 16

Experience a Wee Bit o' Irish at the Old Town Irish Party, 72

SUMMER

Enjoy the Sound of Music at Bohemian Nights, 44

You'll Find the Right Stuff at The Emporium: An American Brasserie, 16

Things Are Just Peachy at the Fort Collins Peach Festival, 80

Spread Beauty at Bloom Flower Market, 131

Experience Smells, Sounds, and Tastes at Taste of Fort Collins, 10

FALL

You'll Find the Right Stuff at The Emporium: An American Brasserie, 16

Spread Beauty at Bloom Flower Market, 131

Get Your Two Wheelin' Fun On at New Belgium's Tour de Fat, 33

Have a Furiliscious Good Time at Tour de Corgi, 92

Let it Go at the Fort Collins Water Lantern Festival, 93

WINTER

You'll Find the Right Stuff at The Emporium: An American Brasserie, 17

Light Up the Holidays at the Downtown Lighting Ceremony, 88

• •

Photo courtesy of Pixabay

INDEX

• •

• •

• •